OLD MAN OF THE MOUNTAIN

THE WEST VIRGINIA BIGFOOT

LES O'DELL

Front cover artwork by Mark A. Randall

Published in partnership with the
West Virginia Bigfoot Museum
Sutton, West Virginia
www.wvbigfootmuseum.com

35th Star Publishing
Charleston, West Virginia
www.35thstar.com

ISBN-13: 979-8-9865993-9-7
Library of Congress Control Number: 2023936393

35th Star Publishing
Charleston, West Virginia
www.35thstar.com

Front cover artwork by Mark A. Randall
Design consulting provided by Studio 6 Sense
Interior design by 35th Star Publishing

Foreword

Here at the West Virginia Bigfoot Museum, we are honored to have Les O'Dell as our top researcher on all things Bigfoot. We appreciate his years of research and fantastic dedication and willingness to share his work. As a native West Virginian, Les loves the Appalachian woods. He inherited that love from his father and is passing it on to his four sons. Les has an ability to not only recognize Hominid footprints but is also more than willing to debunk misleading ones. He is a great woodsman and puts people at ease with his approachable style. In the following pages you will find the copy of his interviews from all over the state of West Virginia. They are written as the words were spoken. We hope you enjoy!

West Virginia Bigfoot Museum
Sutton, West Virginia
www.wvbigfootmuseum.com

West Virginia Bigfoot Museum
400 4th Street, Sutton, West Virginia
www.wvbigfootmuseum.com

Les O'Dell

Follow Les O'Dell on Facebook:
https://www.facebook.com/wvcryptidsandstrangeencounters/

Table of Contents

Introduction

Big·foot
·bigfoot/
Noun: a large, hairy, apelike creature resembling a yeti, supposedly found in northwestern America

Yet·i
·yede/
Noun: yeti; plural noun: yetis
A large hairy creature resembling a human or bear, said to live in the highest part of the Himalayas. Origin:1930s: from Tibetan yeh-teh 'little manlike animal.'

Sas·quatch
·saskwaCH,-kwaCH/
Noun: Sasquatch; plural noun: Sasquatches
Another term for Bigfoot. Origin: Early 20th century: Salish sesqlac.

Other Names for this elusive creature are:
"Protector of the Forest"
"Skunk Ape"
"Old Man of the Mountain"
"Stone Man"
"Yowee"
"Wild Man"

1

In North American folklore, Bigfoot or Sasquatch is a hairy, upright-walking, ape-like creature who reportedly dwells in the wilderness and leaves behind footprints. Although strongly associated with the Pacific Northwest, particularly Oregon, Washington and British Columbia, individuals claim to see the creature all across North America. Every state but Hawaii has legends of or recent sightings of this type of creature.

Most witnesses describe it as a large, hairy, muscular, bipedal ape-like creature, roughly 6-9 feet (1.8-2.7 m) in height, covered in hair described as black, dark brown, or dark reddish and occasionally grayish.

According to David Daegling, the legends existed before there was a single name for the creature. They differed in their details both regionally and between families in the same community.

Ecologist Robert Pyle argues that most cultures have accounts of human-like giants in their folk history, expressing a need for...some larger-than-life creature.

Each language had its own name for the creature featured in the local version of such legends. Many names meant something along the lines of "wild man" or "hairy man," although other names described common actions that it was said to perform, such as eating clams or shaking trees.

Chief Mischelle of the Nlaka'pamux at Lytton, British Columbia, told such a story to Charles Hill-Tout in 1898; he named the creature by a Salishan variant meaning...the benign-faced-one.

Members of the Lummi tell tales about Ts'emekwes, the local version of Bigfoot. The stories are similar to each other in the general descriptions of Ts'emekwes, but details differed among various family accounts concerning the creature's diet and activities. Some regional versions tell of more threatening creatures. The stiyaha or kwi-kwiyai were a nocturnal race. Children were warned against saying the names, lest the monsters hear and come to carry off a person - sometimes to be killed. (1847, Paul Kane)

There are reported stories by the Indians about "Skoocooms," a race of cannibalistic wildmen living on the peak of Mount St. Helens in southern Washington State.

Less-menacing versions have also been recorded, such as one by Reverend Elkanah Walker in 1840. Walker was a Protestant missionary who recorded stories of giants among the Indians living near Spokane, Washington. The Indians said that these giants lived on and around the peaks of nearby mountains and stole salmon from the fishermen's nets.

In the 1920s, Indian Agent J. W. Burns compiled local stories and published them in a series of Canadian newspaper articles. They were accounts told to him by the Sts'Ailes people of Chehalis. The Sts'Ailes and other regional tribes maintained that the Sasquatch were real. They were offended by people telling them that the figures were legendary. According to Sts'Ailes accounts, the Sasquatch preferred to avoid white men and spoke the Lillooet language of the people at Port Douglas, British Columbia, at the head of Harrison Lake. These accounts were published again in 1940. Burns borrowed the term Sasquatch from the Halkomelem sasq'ets and used it in his articles to describe the type of creature portrayed in the local stories.

Stone Man

In West Virginia, it's the legend of the Stone Man.

Early settlers to the area encountered enormous apes that would throw rocks at their camps, and later at their houses. The local Cherokee Indians called the tall human-like creatures Nun'Yunu'Wi, which means "Stone Man" because no weapon could pierce its skin.

Adventurers and later timber men encountered the Stone Man much more often than they would like. Apparently, people still are encountering the Stone Man in West Virginia, to the tune of one hundred reports per year. Examples include this report investigated by the Bigfoot Field Research Organization:

In 2009, a timber worker was cutting down a tree when he noticed a black figure standing further back in the forest. Although he first thought it was a bear standing on its hind legs, the creature raised its left arm to lean against a tree. After a few minutes, it turned and walked into the forest like a man. The timber man saw the creature a year later squatting over a puddle, scooping up water in its hand to drink.

The Stone Man of Appalachia

Bigfoot, or Sasquatch, is ancient history in the Appalachian Mountains. Throughout Appalachia, Native American tribes including the Cherokee, Delaware, Iroquois, Mingo, Seneca, and Shawnee long ago, in variations, named the man-like being who lived alongside them.

The Cherokee in the southern Appalachians named him The Stone Man Nun'yunu'wi. To the north, the Onondagas of the Iroquois nation called the being, "ot-ne-yar-hed" or The Stanish Giant. Other tribes said the being was, "He who is dressed in stone." To all Appalachian tribes, The Stone Man had a reputation for three things: he possessed magical powers; he was a trickster who enjoyed "playing" with humans; and, as with many "Big Man" legends in tribes across the continent, The Stone Man was a cannibal, a monster.

To confirm Stone Man as a cannibal is problematic. However, he seems to have served the useful purpose of being the Appalachian "boogeyman" for Native American parents of small children. He was the monster who, if they wandered far, might seize them and carry them away to his rocky lair.

Eyewitness Accounts

8   Old Man of the Mountain

Sighting in Boone County, 1998

Shared by WV C.A.S.E follower Jamie Lynn Amick
Year: 1998
Nearest Town: Whitesville, WV
Nearest Road: Seng Creek Rd
Nearest Waterway: Believed to be Coal River

Subject Description:
Its face, the eyes were blackish red. But more black than red. The head is cone shaped like a gorilla. The face was really flat looking. The fur was reddish black dirty and matted looking.

Would you say in your opinion it was a Bigfoot?
YES FOR SURE!!! There's NO Doubt About It!!!

Did it make any sound?
No it stood frozen and as we were backing away it went on cross the road.

How has it changed you seeing it?
Well when I go to visit my mom I don't go out at night and I leave before night time. I've always believed in them but seeing one was the scariest thing I've ever seen. And to know that it didn't want to hurt us and us being more scared of it than him of us was very assuring cause as big as it was it could've hurt us.

You said him. Could you tell for sure it was a him or did it just have that feeling?
I just had a feeling cause it was pretty big and really tall. So we called it a him.

Sighting in Boone County, 2014 and 2015

Sent in by WV C.A.S.E follower Shannon Maynard
Year: May 2014 and March 2015
County: Boone
Nearest Town: Comfort, WV
Nearest Road: Joes Creek Rd.
Nearest Water Source: Big Coal River and Joes Creek

Witnesses Description:
I just seen the back of it, buttock and back legs. It looked like muscle on top of muscle. It had reddish brown hair from what I could tell and maybe a little over 7 feet tall. It looked like it had no neck, massive shoulders and when it ran its gate was huge. It looked like a man in shape but also looked like it could rip the roof off a car if it wanted to, massively strong looking.

Four years ago across from my house, just after 4 am, two dogs where barking. I woke up, shined my flashlight and screamed "shut up." That's when I seen a large hairy muscular figure, muscle on top of muscle, it looked like it bolted up the mountain. It looked to be about 7 feet tall or more.

My children seen it the spring before I seen it. But me and a pastor friend just laughed at our kids. They were playing spot light and seen it in the pines. Then I seen it the next year in March. I even got one decent pic of a footprint later on that morning when it became day light. Ever since then from time to time we hear what they call wood knocks and screams like howler monkeys that you hear on a wildlife show. I've heard them before but thought it was a bird imitating something. But I don't think there is any other local animal that can do this.

Additional Witness Comment:
At one time I didn't want people to know for fear thinking I was crazy. But I see there is more people than just me that have seen something like it in West Virginia.

Sighting in Braxton County, 1988 or 1989

Sent in by a WV C.A.S.E follower who we will call "Sam" for privacy reasons.
Year: 1988 or 1989
Month: November during deer season
County: Braxton
Nearest Town: Sutton
Nearest Road: Meadow Lane
Nearest Water Source: Flatwoods Run and Sutton Lake

Witness Description:
What I saw, I will never forget as long as I live... This thing was tall - at least 7 foot. Had the face of almost a man and monkey combined. Big stature that looked like "Andrea the Giant" covered in fur. Body-wise, not the face. The color was a variation of dark and light brown not really a solid. I'll never forget the smell, like mildewed wet dog.

How has your sighting impacted your life?
Chilled me to the bone when I was a kid and had nightmares for weeks. Now this has been 20 plus years ago and to this day I refuse to go in the woods alone or without some sort of protection.

I was in W.V. at my grandmas place hunting with my cousins - sitting on an old oak log - didn't see anything all morning long. It was starting to get warm out that day. A little warmer than usual. So I figured I would make my way back up to the house. Before I did I whistled to let everyone know I was leaving the woods. We make a whistle like a whippoorwill so we know one of is on the move. I got no response from anyone. I waited few more minutes and whistled again. Nothing. Ok, now I know they must have gone to the house and just as I'm ready to get up I hear a noise, so I paused. Then I smelled something. All the sudden, I hear a noise, something moving very fast, I drew up my rifle in the direction of the noise and there he was 20 yards out running. He probably ran 100 yards in the blink of an eye. The whole time taking out saplings like tooth picks. Now being only 13 or 14 I still could not bring myself to tell anyone what I saw that day. Now I'm in my mid 40's and have told only some of my family what I saw. My father said that a few years before that he had experienced the same thing in almost the same spot. Then my cousin told me the same thing. Now for years, I thought, "Ok maybe just being young in the woods alone it was a bear or something."

Yet I have never seen a bear run full speed on its hind legs and take only a few steps and cover so much ground. Then after talking to my father I knew what I saw was real. This is something I will never forget. Especially the smell...

An artist rendering. WV C.A.S.E asked witness how close it was to what was seen. He said, "That's exactly what it looked like to me."

Sighting in Braxton County, 1987

Here is another sighting sent in by WV C.A.S.E follower Jami Peters.
County: Braxton
Year: August 1987 at 11:30am
Area: Frametown

Witness Description:
There's a Bigfoot in Braxton County, this I guarantee you. Seven of us seen it in broad day light coming up out of the Little Birch River near Frametown in our family camp.

It was August 1987, 11:30 am, we just got done eating breakfast outside when my aunt heard something. We looked toward the river and up over the river bank came an 8 foot or better Squatch. It walked right through our camp. When it reached the bottom of the mountain there was a gas line right-of-way completely clear. It chose to go up through the woods and not the gas line. My uncle tried to get close enough on an ATV to get a picture but it was too fast as it crossed our property. It never looked at us or paid us any attention, it was going like it was on a mission. It was reddish brown, a cone-shaped head, no neck, and about four feet wide.

The next summer I found signs of where I think this thing may have lived. I found rocks bigger than car hoods stood up on their ends in a creek bed in the middle of nowhere as if it was hunting food.

We don't own it now but I can take you to exactly were it happened. But many times we did hear screams in the night and when you get in to it you're about 7 miles in any direction to another human being. If it rains or snows you don't come out until it dries up or melts off.

Sighting in Greenbrier County, 2009

Date: May 15, 2009
County: Greenbrier County
Location: Near Sam Black Exit, Jones Road, Meadow Bluff

Anonymous Eyewitness Account:
On the night of Friday, May 15, 2009, I went out on the back porch to get some fresh air. I smelled something like a wet dog. When I turned around I saw a seven or eight foot tall creature that was brown, hairy and kind of lanky. As soon as I saw it I gasped and took off running. Then next morning my family and I went outside and began looking around and fount footprints about 14 or 15 inches long, and 4 or 5 feet span between each one in our garden. It appeared to be barefooted and at one point running.

Sighting in Cabell County, 2001

Shared by WV C.A.S.E follower Robin Simms.
Date: July 2001
County: Cabell County

Eyewitness Description:
At the end of July 2001, I was taking a hike on the hill with my kids, my mom and dad, and my brother. We were following a dirt road that runs across the ridge line. On the left of us, the property line is divided with a barbed wire fence. On the right, it slopes downhill, into a cleared off hillside. Then about 50 feet below, multi-flora rose bushes have grown up, then the woods begin.

I am walking about 100 feet ahead of the rest of the family, along with Sarah. Our dog Puff was walking at my side. We hear some rustling in the thorn bushes below us. At first, I'm thinking cows. We have a few head of cattle on the farm, roaming. In addition, we are walking in their "pasture" area. Puff also heard it and perked up, looking over the hillside towards the right. Puff starts barking and takes off down the hill. I know then it is not a cow. Puff doesn't chase cows. Sarah (my daughter) and I then see a head, a hairy head and shoulders standing above the multi-flora rose bushes. It takes off down the hillside towards the trees, with Puff on its heels. Whatever this thing was, it was taller than the bushes (which we later went down and judged them to be at least 8 or 9 feet tall - and this thing stood a head taller than the bushes). It was a reddish brown color.

I have told several family members and friends what we have seen. They think we are crazy. I know there is something out there. I was like most people. I didn't believe in such things. Until I saw it with my own eyes.

Sighting in Greenbrier County, 2014

County: Greenbrier County
Nearest Town: Quinwood
Location: Carl Mountain
Date: September 15, 2014

Eyewitness Account:
On my way to work this evening at 8:46pm. I was driving down the mountain, when I saw what I thought was a bear. I slowed down, just in case it ran out in front of me. When it stepped over the guardrail, I knew it wasn't a bear. I rolled my window up, it turned, looked at me, had my bright lights on, in two steps, crossed a two lane road, then up the mountain. Scared, OMG… Can't believe what I saw. Still shook up! Very dark, that animal was very dark, matted hair, from what I could see in my headlights. My guess, height-wise, close to nine foot. Very tall. Happened on Carl Mountain, near Quinwood, West Virginia.

Sighting in Fayette County, 2007

Date: November 2007
County: Fayette County
Location: New River Gorge area

Eyewitness Account:
To keep it short. I was deer hunting in the New River Gorge in Fayetteville, West Virginia, and it was in 2007, the week of Thanksgiving.

It was evening with about two hours of daylight left and I noticed movement about 60 yards towards the gorge from my position. 1 raised my gun to view the movement through the scope. After holding it in position for 10 seconds or so I saw a very large hand appear from the side of a large poplar tree. It was palm against the tree and I saw fingers mostly. Then to my surprise I saw a head peek from around the large tree and two LARGE eyes affixed on a head of a creature I've never seen before. And I'm a hunter… have been since I was 8… I'm now 38. The Bigfoot blinked twice while looking at me and then stepped back behind the tree. I viewed it for about 20 seconds while it was looking at me. My mind just couldn't figure out what it was and I knew what it wasn't. I had no desire to shoot it and very well could have but my mind and body almost seemed to be in a state of shock while viewing it. I had to cross near the location on the trail out of the woods and I was F'n terrified even with a loaded deer rifle. My hair stood on end when I realized that I would have to go towards the location to get out of the woods. I called my uncle as soon as I got to my jeep and told him. He believed me. I am a VERY honest man and would never lie about this. The thing is though, I never heard it run away or move through the leaves. And you can hear movement from 200+ yards off in these woods. It's like it just disappeared. I came home very shaken from the experience and it changed my life. Now I know that it is out there.

It was very cool looking. About 7 feet tall, it had very dark large pupils and around the pupils its eyes were almost owl like. It had brownish blond fur and it had a visible face. It almost looked like the troll faces that you used to put on your pencils as kids... really... but, it was very clean looking and not what you would expect. Its fingers were long and thick with no fur and it had dark fingernails. I had my scope on 9 power and it was equivalent to being about 30 feet from me visually. It was real and I would take a polygraph and swear on my life.

Vocalizations, 1995

Sent in by a WV C.A.S.E follower who would like to remain anonymous.
Year: 1995
Month: November
Temperature: Cold, low 40's
County: Fayette
Nearest town: Kanawha Falls
Nearest Water Source: Kanawha River
Area: Cotton Hill

Eyewitness Account:
I didn't have a sighting but heard what I believe to be vocalizations of a
Bigfoot. If you repost my story I wish my identity to remain unknown.
The place was Fayette County, on Cotton Hill, across the Kanawha River.
The nearest community is Kanawha Falls. It was November of 1995, the
first week of rifle season for antlered deer. I was 21 years old and had been
hunting this area from the young age of 8 years old. So I know what is in
these woods. Anyway, a few weeks before camp was set up the area was
plentiful with deer and sign of deer. I set up camp on what is called the
river front, went out the morning of the opening day and hunted. I was
in my spot about 30 minutes before daylight and waited as the day went
on - no sign of anything not even a chipmunk! It was about 45 minutes
before dark so I made my way back to camp. I get to camp, build a fire
and by now it's dusk. On a ridge above me came the most horrifying
sound I've ever heard. It started out like a woman scream and continued
on into a deep guttural growl. It lasted maybe 45 seconds then it seemed
to fade away.

I was raised in those woods on Cotton Hill. My dad would take me there
to help cut fire wood to heat our home and we hunt that mountain and
ride ATV's there in the summer. I'm 44 years old - about to turn 45 next

month. I have lived in this area for 42 years other than a deployment to Iraq from 2003 to 2005. I have never heard anything like it. I mean now days coyotes are thick around the area but back then other than bear which would be hibernating or a wild dog there isn't anything that could sound like what I heard.

I've reported it to the BFRO, but I guess it didn't interest them because I've never heard anything back from them. That's been about 3 years ago, but I really could care less if they or anyone else takes me serious. I know it wasn't anything that has been cataloged to this day making that noise.

Additional comments by witness after questioning by WV C.A.S.E
Question: Could you estimate how far away the sound was?
Answer: I know sound travels farther at night but it seemed to be four hundred yards above me on the ridge.

Question: Were there any other sounds in the area. I know you said you didn't see any animal activity in the area but what about sounds?
Answer: No that's the strangest thing about the whole ordeal. The area seemed to be deathly silent.

Question: Have you ever had any other odd experiences in this area other than the scream the one time? Like the feeling of being watched or anything like that?
Answer: Other than that day, in that specific area, no. All that morning was eerie - the silence and the feeling that something wasn't right and like I was being watched. I've been back to the area several times hunting since that year and haven't had anything out of the ordinary happen.

Question: Just to rule this possibility out. Did it sound like a big cat?
Answer: Well according to the West Virginia DNR we don't have any big cats but I have seen and heard them on Deepwater Mountain, an area that route 61 passes over from Montgomery to Oak Hill, and no it wasn't a big cat.

Sighting in Fayette County, 2013

Sent in by a WV C.A.S.E follower who would like to remain anonymous.
Year: 2013
Time of year: It was fall, the week of Thanksgiving
County: Fayette
Nearest road: Rt 60
Nearest town: Lookout

Eyewitness description:
It was close to 6 ½ to 7 foot tall, dark brown to red hair. It had a very smooshed face, almost a flat nose, very dark and the arms stretched past its waistline. It appeared to be eating the remains of a deer.

A few years back I was staying with my best friend. It was the night before rifle season came in and we had gone out to scout where we were going to hunt the next day. Feeling off that morning I still went to my spot and sat down in my stand for the day. About an hour before daybreak something started moving around below me under the ridge past where I couldn't see. This made me feel very uneasy because I felt like I was being watched, which continued until 11am when I finally decided to walk out, get lunch, then return to my stand. As I walked out on a logging road overlooking a bowl down the mountain full of Hollys and brush I started smelling an awful odor. I figured it was an animal or something had died down the hill from me. After eating my lunch I made my way back down the road. Arriving at the bowl the stench was still lingering. I glanced down the hill looking for any sign of a carcass. I noticed a large brown spot in the thicket, so I threw up my rifle to get a better look. I noticed what looked like a bear but a brownish red. Of course we only have black bears so I got very nervous being about 20 at the time and by myself. I started making a commotion to scare it off before getting in my stand, but I got more than I bargained for once it stood up on two legs and shifted its weight to look at me. We made eye contact that felt like it lasted for minutes before it turned away and took off. Within 4 to 5 strides it was out of my view and what I figured to be gone. It was at least 5'5 to 7 foot tall, judging by the trees it was standing beside - what I believe to be a Bigfoot.

Later that night returning back to his house we were in the garage talking about the plans for hunting the next day. It sounded like something was hitting the roof. We walked out 2 or 3 times trying to see or hear anything for about 15 or 20 minutes. It ended up being rocks and sticks hitting the roof of his garage which we found the next day. But finally getting fed up with it we took lights and walked up the hill in the woods beside his garage when something very large started charging at us then turned and ran back up the hill approximately 200 yards from where I had hunted that day.

Additional witness comments.
I never went hunting by myself up there again. I always have the encounter in the back of my mind when I go hunting hoping I don't run into another one. I completely froze in fear when we saw each other, though I was armed and had sights on him. I've only told 2 or 3 people about the encounter and they called me crazy, that wasn't what I saw. But to this day I know that was no normal animal. My best friend has had experiences with it other than that day but he refuses to talk about them. About 4 years ago they started logging up there and he said the encounters stopped soon after.

Witness was asked to pick a face from a random group of pics I put together.
This is the one that was chosen and witness comment:
"This one almost exactly! Just a little darker face but yes, that one."

Sighting in Cabell County, 2012

Sent in by a WV C.A.S.E follower who would like to remain anonymous.
Date: August 2012
County: Cabell
Location: Between Barboursville and Huntington

Eyewitness Account:
I live in Cabell County. I was coming home late one night after work. It was August of 2012. I was working the 2nd shift that night. It was just after 11pm when I was driving home on Rt. 60. I remember it being hot that night. I had my AC up. I was in Barboursville. Heading towards Huntington, but I live in Barboursville. Anyways, coming from left to right, I saw a gigantic figure cross the road. I stopped.

No one was behind me at the time. I didn't see its face. It was above my car. In my headlights, I saw reddish brown hair. In one motion, it cleared the turning lane and was off the road to the right. I turned into my subdivision, stopped, and rolled down my passenger side window. It was probably not the smartest idea at the time. I didn't see anything. Granted, it was dark and after 11. However, whatever that was, went down a man-made stone wall creek bed, in the creek. I don't know anyone who would attempt that in daylight, let alone night time. I can't swear it was a Bigfoot. I don't know what it was. It was big and walked on 2 legs.

Sighting in Harrison County, 1974

Season: Spring
Date: 5/01/1974
County: Harrison County
Nearest Town: Stonewood
Nearest Road: Old Logging Road

Witness Account:
This is the story as was relayed to the investigator. Just after dark the witness, who was 15 at the time, and his friend were getting nightcrawlers to go fishing with. Just behind their house, which like many West Virginia houses is rural, there was an old logging road which was covered by very heavy green briars. The witness heard something coming down the mountain through the green briars. He shined his flashlight and saw an enormous animal which was built like a large bodybuilder. He watched the animal from 60 feet away traveling right to left. He watched the animal for several seconds. What stuck out in his memory the most was the swinging arms and the hair 10-12 inches long hanging down off of the forearms. The hair in general was mostly straight and dark brown in color with reddish tinge on tips. It really scared his friend and him. The next day based on a sapling they estimated the animal to be 9 feet tall.

"Mystery of Margaret"

This is a story shared with me by an older gentleman who would like to remain anonymous.
County: Harrison
Location: Margaret

Eyewitness Account:
What I'm about to tell you happened more than forty years ago. I was fresh out of the Vietnam War and living on our family farm in a little backwoods community called Margaret in Harrison County. I was at the farm watching some of my nieces and nephews. The water in the house had stopped running. So I told one of my nephews to go to the cellar where the pump for the water well was located. The entrance to the cellar was on the outside of the house. You had to go down stairs at the back of the house, walk to the back wall near the far corner of the house, then walk down another set of steps to the cellar.

My nephew was afraid to go alone but I had to stay with the other younger kids. So I told him I would stand at the back door to keep an eye on him and he had nothing to be afraid of. Boy was that about to change. As he walked to the second set of steps and started down toward the cellar, a huge arm about six feet off the ground, with a large five fingered hand and covered in long reddish hair reached around the corner of the house like it was about to grab his head. I screamed at him to watch out. He turned just in time to see the arm being pulled back around the corner. He then screamed, jumped and ran back to the doorway where I was standing. I did not see anything other than the arm. I can't say what it was I seen but after time and hearing other stories over the years… Although I never experienced anything like it again while living on the farm which was sold some years later, I can only speculate it was a Bigfoot or something like it.

Sighting in Jackson County

County: Jackson
Date: ?

Eyewitness Account:
I have a story that happened in Jackson Co. About thirty years ago we bought an abandoned farm on Gay Road. Our son, then about 11, had been playing in the creek and he came home scared to death. He said when he climbed up the creek bank something big and hairy was standing up watching him. I asked if it was a bear and he said, "No, it was Bigfoot." I asked if it was a large coon and he again said, "No it was Bigfoot." He was obviously very shaken. I asked him if it was the old man who used to own the property, and he said empathetically, "It was Bigfoot!" Recently I asked him what he really saw, thinking he would own up to mom after all this time, but he just said, "It was Bigfoot!"

Sighting in Kanawha County, Late 1990s

Sent in by a WV C.A.S.E follower who would like to remain anonymous.
Date: Late 1990s
Time of year: Fall
Time of day: around 2pm
County: Kanawha County
Location: Hughes Creek area

Witness comment:
Hughes Creek is between London and Riverside. Then you have Glasgow
and Cedar Grove. U.S. route 60. Hugheston is a part of Hughes Creek.
It's across the four lane.

Witness description:
It was between 7 and 8 feet tall. Its hair wasn't thick, I could see the
skin. I remember a few wrinkles on the forehead and its facial expression
was like mad or confusing like. I could see that it was a male. Its chest
muscles were huge. Its shoulders were huge and its thighs and legs were
very toned and big. It didn't have a neck. Its head was big and it looked
like its head sat right on those big shoulders.

I had an encounter with something that I can't explain back in the late
90s. It took place in eastern Kanawha County in West Virginia. A friend
and myself were riding dirt bikes on the mountain up Hughes Creek. We
were on an old logging road up Cobb Holler. I was ahead of my friend a
couple minutes due to him stopping for some reason. It was about 2 in the
afternoon on a Fall day and the sky was blue and the sun was bright. As
I topped the hill on the road we were on, I saw something in the middle
of the road that at first I thought was a black bear. It was about 100 yards
from me and I was looking down at it from the hill that dropped down
and went right where it was before curving and going back up the other

side. I turned my bike off and as soon as I did it stood up and turned towards me. It was at this time that I knew that I was not looking at a bear. I could see the skin shining through the hair and I could see the muscles and the face which was human-ape like. It didn't have a snout like a black bear does. It was very broad shouldered and its buttocks was like a human. Its arms hung way past its waist and I couldn't believe that I was looking at this. My friend was coming up the hill behind me at this time on his 2 stroke motorcycle that was loud. It startled this thing which then turned away from us and ran about 30 yards toward the valley on the left of where we were. There was a tree on the ground and this thing jumped over the fallen tree on two legs before jumping over the hill. My friend saw it running away and jumping over the hill and he asked me, "What was that?" I told him what I had just witnessed and he insisted that we get out of there.

I grew up in West Virginia my whole life and have always been an avid outdoorsman who hunted every year with family and friends. I've seen hundreds of bear and this thing was huge. It was big enough to reach down and grab a small pickup truck and flip it over. When it ran away, it was amazing watching it jump the tree and jump into briar patch filled weeds. That hill was straight up and down where it went.

Additional comments, after some questions by WV C.A.S.E
Question: Did it show any facial expressions?
Answer: It stood up and turned towards me with a look that it wasn't scared of me at all. It almost looked like it was sizing me up or trying to find out what I was.

Question: Did it make any sounds?
Answer: It didn't make any sound. It just started at me and turned away and ran when my buddy came up behind me.

Question: A lot of people that see these things say, 'it looked at me like to say you are not supposed to be here.' Did it give you that feeling?

Answer: Yeah and I got the feeling that it was deciding on what it needed to do to me to ensure that he was going home. I guess I was far enough away from him that he didn't feel like I was a threat to him. He could have grabbed me and my bike and drug us off. I've never gone into the woods without a firearm since then. It's haunted my thoughts for 20 years.

Question: How did it make you feel to see something that is not supposed to exist?
Answer: I know that I saw it and I think that there are more things that exist than we know. It makes me feel a few different ways to be honest. Scared of the unknown, intrigued by the reality of more than we can explain is out there. Mad because I know it's out there but can't prove it."

Sighting in Lincoln County, 2011

Sent in by a WV C.A.S.E follower who would like to remain anonymous.
County: Lincoln County
Date: Approximately 2011

Witness Account:
I'd like to tell you about an encounter I had with a Bigfoot but please keep me anonymous. This happened about ten years ago close to Branchland in Lincoln County. I was helping my brother. He had timbered a large part of his property and was then cutting it up into lumber in order to build his house. The sawmill was one of the portable, trailer type mills and he wanted me to keep watch over it so that it wouldn't get stolen. So I was staying in his RV camper and watching over the sawmill. There wasn't much to do up there so each night me and my dog would go out and sit around a campfire. We had been doing the same routine for several months and most nights were quiet. Occasionally we got visited by an opossum or raccoon. Once we even had a group of coon hunters come up and say hi.

So it was getting on around the start of January - it was a very cold and clear night but it was pretty nice sitting by the fire. My dog alerted me that something was approaching our camp. He didn't bark but let out kind of a very low growl and all of the hackles on his back stood up. Pretty soon I could hear something heavy crunching through the leaves, walking up the hill straight towards us. I remember thinking that it was probably another dog or maybe a person. A few minutes later it walked up to the edge of the fire light. Just opposite of me and my dog. It just stood there staring at us. It was about 8 feet tall and solid muscle. I could see it pretty well in the flickering fire light and it very much resembled the silverback that I had seen at the zoo a few years before. Similar yet different. Its face was too flat and it's back too straight. It had walked in a perfect bipedal fashion. It was too human like. I was absolutely frozen to the spot in fear. As was my dog who didn't react other than he continued to emit low growls and his hackles never went down. The Sasquatch slowly squatted down onto its haunches and very, very slowly it reached out with one arm and moved a sapling aside, as if it wanted a better look at me. Squatted down we were about at eye level with each other and we just stared at each other for what seemed like an eternity although it probably only lasted no more than twenty seconds. Then it quickly released the sapling and stood up, looked away, looked back at me and my dog one more time and then took off down the hill at a brisk pace. Just like that it was gone. I will never forget this event.

I can still remember it like it was yesterday. I told my brother and he laughed at me, as have most other people I've told. I tend not to talk about it much anymore and honestly, I would possibly consider that I was just "seeing things" except that my dog saw it and reacted to it.

A few months later I was fairly consumed with the encounter and I discovered the BFRO website. I found an encounter that was reported on there from a few years before. It was from a family just on the other side of the county border. They were in Wayne County but very close to where my brother's property is. And they had reported a few sightings of a Bigfoot and also rocks being thrown at their house in the middle of the night. This coupled with my own experience turned a definite skeptic into a definite believer. Thank you for providing a place where people can share their experiences, keep up the good work!

Sighting in Greenbrier County, 2010

Date: Nov 2010
Location: Sherwood Lake Area
County: Greenbrier

Witness Account:
I guess I should start off saying I have always been skeptical about the whole Bigfoot thing. Reason being I've spent 40 years in the outdoors hunting and fishing. And I only heard stories, never experienced anything out of the ordinary that couldn't be explained - until this happened to me.

So here it is. I've hunted and fished in the area leading into Sherwood Lake for many, many years. I'm not exactly sure the distance from the lake, possibly three miles. I can tell you I was camped about 1/4 mile below Dilley Run Trail. I know the area extremely well and it's a fairly remote wilderness area. I've spent a lot of time there alone and have never felt strange or as if something wasn't right - until November of 2010.

It was the week before our traditional bucks-only deer season, which was the week before Thanksgiving. I had decided to take two weeks vacation to go up to bow hunt and get a better idea where to tag my buck with my rifle the following week. Well, the first few days I was there bow hunting, everything seemed as usual. I was seeing deer and other wildlife. Then on Thursday early morning while walking back into the same area I'd been hunting all week, early before daylight, (Note this area is a good 2 1/2 to 3 miles from the nearest road) I had an uneasy feeling all the way to my stand site, almost like I could feel the presence of something following me. I shook it off and made it to my hunting spot and set up. Around 7:30am I heard a sound I'd heard before but only on TV. At first I thought, no that wasn't what I thought it was. Then I heard it again and I knew 100% it was a wood knock! But then it grew silent. Then like 15 minutes later I heard it again further down the hollow from the direction I'd came in at. The rest of that day was non-eventful. By non-eventful I mean I never heard anything again! Not a wood knock, not a bird, not a squirrel and I never seen a deer! I was kinda at a loss for what to do about what I'd heard, really nothing I could do. That evening I made sure I was out of the mountains and back to my camper before dark.

That night I built a fire and was listening to some bluegrass music for a couple of hours beside my camper. I started noticing lightning flashes so finally decided it was time to turn in. So I started getting things ready for bed. I went to my truck and turned off the music, then went in my camper to fix my bed up. It may have been an hour later when I heard thunder and it began to storm pretty bad. With the rain on that camper roof it wasn't long before I was asleep. I'm not sure how long I was asleep before being awakened by a loud bang to the camper! It scared me to death, I jumped almost outta bed. I grew deathly quiet. I really thought a tree or something had hit the camper because of the storm. But the storm was all over with and gone. I was getting dressed to go see if a limb or tree had hit the camper when I heard another very loud and distinguished wood knock! It was a wood knock! And it wasn't but maybe a hundred yards away, back behind my camper in the hollow I came out of that evening. I won't lie - it scared me! I immediately got my pistol out and my rifle loaded and laid them very close to me. Cause I knew in my mind for sure what I was hearing and I knew what was making them sounds. I'll also note this was the week before the gun rifle season. There was no one else camped near me or really anywhere at this time. I never heard anything else that night but had a truly hard time going to sleep.

Well, the next morning when the alarm went off I wasn't really certain I wanted to go back in the mountains before daylight. I didn't - I stayed in the camper till it got daylight. I decide then I'd go see what had hit the camper. I went out and got up in back of my truck so I could see the top of the camper thinking still a limb had fell on top of the camper. There was nothing there. I then began to walk around the camper, and on the backside there was a pretty sizable dent in the camper. On the ground next to the camper was a rock bigger than a softball but not as big as a football. I picked it up and sized it up with the dent in the camper and it was very obvious the rock made that dent. I had deep thoughts about packing up and leaving. But I kept telling myself how many times I'd been in these same mountains in the middle of the night chasing coon dogs, way before daylight to go deer hunting and long deer drags out well after dark and had never had a bad experience.

As crazy as it sounds I convinced myself to stay. So later that day I grabbed my stuff and off I went to my hunting spot. I got within a half mile of where I'd been going and decided because I was late getting in, I'd just set up at a different location. I got a spot cleaned up, sat down and started observing my surroundings of what I could see. I was just above a creek bed about 100 yards in a sizable open area surrounded on three side by a huge thicket. I notice a huge black stump across the hollow on a small point. Again, it was deathly quiet. I sat for a few hours, then I decided I didn't really want to walk out of there in the dark. So I started to walk down the ridge back to the trail when movement across the hollow on the ridge where the big stump was caught my eye. I was amazed and dumbfounded at what I was seeing! The stump was gone and the movement was something walking on two legs with very wide shoulders and long arms. It was rusty reddish brown with long hair. I really couldn't tell much about its face from the distance we were apart. It was a Bigfoot! I'm 100% sure of what I was seeing! I've seen many, many bear, but this wasn't a bear - it was huge! I guess at least 8 feet tall. And what really got me was that huge stump was gone! So what I was now seeing had been what I thought was a stump. It sat there for close to 4 hours and watched me! I'm sure of it. I was beside myself freaked out! And I still had a 2 mile walk back to my camp. I think that was the fastest I ever came out of there. I got back to camp, but I was still shaking and definitely in a state of shock. I put my stuff in the truck and drove to White Sulphur Springs that night. I stayed there at a small motel, trying to figure out what I should do. That morning I decided I'd had enough of Sherwood for this year. I headed back to get my camper to leave.

Upon getting closer to the camper, I came by a few camp sites where there was now a few camps being set up and a bit more activity of people in the area. Once at the camper another camper had set up just below me. There were two guys there. I got out and opened up my camper when I noticed the two men coming my way walking. Note I was still pretty in shock about what I'd experienced the last few days. They introduced themselves and went to asking "how long I'd been there and was I seeing deer?" Just hunting related questions. In a short time they headed back to their camp. With everyone else around I again reassured myself I should stay and get ready for opening of the rifle season on the coming Monday.

So everything did settle down including my nerves a bit. On Monday morning I sprang outta bed extremely early so I could get to my stand very early. Hoping the other hunters would push me a deer. I was in my stand well before daylight. That's when I hear the bone-chilling, goosebumps, hair-standing-up sound. It was in my opinion no doubt the sound of a Bigfoot hollering. It's hard to explain the sound in a message but it was like a "woooowooooo." It done it two times spaced out like maybe 30 seconds apart. I know what I heard and I've never heard another animal in my whole life make that sound in those mountains. It got silent till about 7:15am when I heard it again on up the ridge maybe a half mile from where I'd heard it the first time. Note I was way up on the mountain in a tree stand, so I could look down and see the whole valley and a couple of big ridges that came off the Allegheny Mountain Trail that fell into the valley where we camped.

The ridge the sounds were coming from came up out of that swamp and headed toward what's the Meadow Mountain Trail. I listened to it make them calls three more times as it continued up that long ridge, until it dropped over the backside of the Meadow Mountain Trail. I killed a deer later that morning, packed up and left. I hate to admit it, but I've never been back there since to hunt or fish. I've never experienced anything like that before this or ever really thought I would. I do know what I experienced over that time period and no one will ever convince me otherwise what I heard or saw, wasn't a Bigfoot! I only told this to my wife when I got home and it was a few years later before I ever told anyone else. I've only repeated this story to maybe 4 people total - just figured others would say he's crazy. But again, I never was a believer in Bigfoot. But I know now for a fact what I seen and experienced leaves no doubt in my mind what it was. I experienced a Bigfoot on not one but a few different occasions over that time period.

Sighting in Logan County

County: Logan County

Witness Account:
I had walked down to the game room about five minutes below my house (which is on a hill up against a mountain). Around 11-11:30pm, as I started walking back home, I heard some kind of a loud noise like a woman screaming. I spotted something on the mountain standing beside the light pole on the other end of my home. When I got to the top of my hill I froze in fear not knowing what it was, and it just watched me. About ten minutes later my neighbor (which has a 2-story home) seen me just standing there. He said he knew something was wrong because I would not answer him when he hollered at me.

I saw the tall dark thing looking towards my neighbor's house. I ran behind our building outside, but I could still see it. It kept standing there. About five minutes had gone by and my neighbor has his gun running up the hill to see what was wrong. That thing seen him and turned and ran/walked back onto the mountain. I was so terrified, and it had scared my dog so bad that she hid under my neighbor's porch.

Finally, my neighbor got on the hill where I was at and I explained to him what I saw. It was about 9-10 feet tall, long dark fur from head to toe, and it walked/ran in long strides. My dad and Roger (neighbor) tells me to get in the house. They have their guns and they seen footprints about 18 to 20 inches long or more. The weeds and limbs on the trees were torn off as if someone had taken a weed-whacker to them.

The next night my neighbor was laying down in his daughter's room on the couch watching her, when all of a sudden something hit his sliding doors so hard that it knocked his curtain rods and all down. He grabbed his gun, goes outside and did not see anything. He puts the curtains back up and goes to see if he can hit the doors and knock the curtains down. He could not hit it hard enough, so he said whatever it was had to be at least nine or ten feet tall to be able knock them down. He saw the same footprints in his yard the next morning.

Sighting in Lincoln County, 1998

Shared by a WV C.A.S.E follower who would like to remain anonymous.
Year: 1998
Time of Year: Spring
Closest Town: Midkiff
Closest Body of Water: Mud River

Subject description:
8 feet tall, hands and feet like a human with long white hair. Its face looked like a man's face but more wrinkled with a protruding nose and white hair surrounding it. The eyes were a light color. I use to always say ice blue if that makes sense. Almost like glass with a hint of blue.

Eyewitness Encounter:
My first encounter would be around 1998. I was 16. Me, my mom, step dad and siblings were out hunting molly moochers (morel mushrooms). We were headed back towards the car when I was a little ways ahead of them. I yelled back that I was gonna go down the other hill by the car and look. They were with the smaller children so it was fine.

As I started down the path I could smell this awful smell. It kept getting stronger and stronger. I put my shirt up over my face to try and cap the horrible odor. As I'm walking and looking at the ground for mushrooms I hear a grunt kinda sound. I really can't explain it but I looked up and didn't see anything so I kept looking but this smell kept getting worse. I couldn't help but feel as if I was being watched! I walked very slow hoping my mom and family would catch up soon because I was a little scared! I heard the sound again and a tree limb or something snap! I slowly looked forward where the sound was coming from and maybe 5 feet in front of me was a big tree. On each side of this tree at the bottom I seen two feet covered in long dirty white hair. I looked up the tree slowly - I was shaking to death at this point. Its arms were wrapped around the tree as if it was hugging the tree. It peeked its head out and made the sound again. I stood there frozen just staring at this creature for what seemed like forever! I got a really good look at it before I ran like a chicken with its head cut off! Its face was white, wrinkly even - had hands like a human and feet like a human but with really long dirty white hair. This thing stood every bit of 8 feet and I believe if it wanted to harm me it very could have.

By the time I made it to the top of the hill I was crying and begging to leave! My family could smell the awful smell and could hear the noise it made. We hear it walking away because of sticks breaking loudly! I've seen it several times after that also!

Other information after questioning witness:
Question: Do you feel what you saw was a Bigfoot?
Answer: Most definitely believe it was.

Question: How did it change you after seeing it?
Answer: I believe there is things in these woods that we have no idea about!

Sighting in Logan County, 1996

Sent in by WV C.A.S.E follower Tammy Hensley
Year: 1996
Time of Year: Fall
Time of day: 1:30 pm
Nearest Town: Oceana
County: Logan
Nearest Road: Rt. 10
Nearest Water Source: Guyandotte River
Distance Between Witness and Creature: Approximately 60 yards
Duration of Sighting: Approximately 3-4 minutes

Witness description of creature:
7 foot tall. Medium light brown in color. Walked upright. Arms longer than a man's, hung to the knees. Shoulders and neck shaped like a mans but larger.

WV C.A.S.E: Could it have been a bear?
Witness: No way. My husband thought it might of been but it wasn't a bear.

Witness sighting:
I lived at 3 Mile Curve in a very wooded area not too far from Oceana. There were only two houses, mine and my in laws. Around 1996 I was alone, my husband was at work and my son in school. It was around 1:30 pm. I looked out of the bedroom window toward the mountain. I saw a large medium brown color creature that stood upright and walked like a man. He was walking very fast swinging his arms at his side. Then he started to climb up the mountain. He climbed like no man could. It was a steep spot and you would have to stoop over and hold onto limbs or tall grass to climb it but he walked upright without stooping or holding

on to anything and in a few seconds he was gone. I lived there 32 years and that was the first and only time I saw him. I told my husband and son later that day when they got home but they thought it probably was a bear. But it was no bear. I didn't hear it, I was inside.

Sighting in Marion County, 60 years ago

County: Marion County
Location: Fairmont

I (Les O'Dell) was told a story about a Bigfoot sighting by a lady that is 73 years old. Here's the story:

I was 13 years old and lived in a row of log cabins along the river in Fairmont. My father and uncles all worked in the local mines.

One night we all piled into the old car my father owned and went to the Lazy A drive-in. On the way home we turned down the road leading to our old log cabin. Me and the other kids in the car noticed a large, upright walking, hairy animal over 6 feet tall, walking on the hillside alongside the car. It walked along the car for a good distance. My father said it had to be a black bear. I know that black bear can walk on their hind feet but this thing never went down on all four feet at any time like a bear would. I know what I saw and to this day I still can remember clearly what I saw!

[Following page: Contemporary photos taken in the area of the Fairmont sighting.]

Contemporary photos taken in the area of the Fairmont sighting

Sighting in Marion County, 1921

Shared by WV C.A.S.E follower Todd Hulsey.
What really interests me about this story, besides the story itself, is how long ago it took place. This was well before Bigfoot was even called Bigfoot and even nearly half a century before the Petterson-Gimlin film.

County: Marion County
Year: Approx 1921
Nearest town: Metz
Nearest road: States Fork
Type of area: Forrest and farmland

Account:
My grandma told me a story about an "ape" that was running on two legs between her mother's house and the barn while they were kids on the porch. Her dad grabbed the gun and pursued it but she said it ran so fast he couldn't get a shot. She said it was as tall as the top of the window. Her mom wondered if a circus lost the gorilla, but my grandma said it looked like a giant hairy man. This happened on State's Fork Road in Marion County. My family owns 600 acres at the head of the hollow there and we still have two log homes from very early 1800s. I have three such stories of that area. I know my grandparents had never heard of Bigfoot and when I was a kid, I hadn't either, but when we walked the farm my pap would point things like this out to me. My grandfather has a similar story of the ape-man that he and his dad saw while out installing fence line. It was in one valley over.

My grandma passed in 2015 at the age of 93. Her mom, my great grandma, lived until she was 98. My uncle who was a little boy on the porch is still alive. He is 98.

Encounters in Mason County, 2018

Sent in by a WV C.A.S.E follower who would like to remain anonymous.
Date: 2018
Nearest town: Point Pleasant
Nearest water source: Ohio River

Eyewitness Account:
I go out to feed my horses and mind you, the stalls are close to the hillside
and I had my back to that pasture and tree line when as I was fumbling
with the stall latch. There was this loud yowl that made the hair on the
back of my neck stand up and my usually docile mare started flipping out.
It scared me so bad that I scaled the door and climbed in the window and
hid in the back corner as my mare was at the front of the stall with ears
pinned. I called my mom on my cell but by the time my brother and dad
got out there, my mare calmed down. My uncle's dog that was loose on
the property at the time did not leave from under the house the whole day
and kept watching the hillside. While patrolling, my dad found a print
at the top of the hill that really spooked him. It wasn't a cat or a canine,
but more of a "large ape, almost human".

Now, about a week later, stuff changed. My dad was heading home
through the TNT area one night when he smelled a "dirty, nasty, musty"
smell he had smelled during a Bigfoot encounter back when he was in
basic in Washington state. He came across a group of coon hunters with
spooked dogs and they were all shook up. So, around Christmas, everyone
started smelling this really off odor, my brother seen a large humanoid
figure in the woods along the road about 600 feet from my horse pasture,
eerie "being watched" feelings, and the horses acting uneasy. Things have
died down now, but there are still evenings where something feels off and
those instincts start kicking in to not go hike in the woods.

Sightings in Monongalia and Preston Counties, 2004 and 2005

Sent in by WV C.A.S.E follower Richard Ripley of encounters that he experienced.
Date: 2004 and 2005
County: Monongahela and Preston Counties

Eyewitness Account:
I am new to this page. I have 4 separate sasquatch encounters dating back since 2004 in Monongalia and Preston Counties.

First encounter was at the dead end of a West Virginia road in the woods owned by BoParc at the edge of the wood line. I was 16 years old sitting on my front porch steps at around 6:30 am when I seen what at first appeared to be a large man dressed in black. However upon closer examination it was a black furred bipedal that stood over 8 foot. (I measured most recently the point at which the top of his head peaked at.) It stood there, stared at me for several chilling minutes before he or she just turned around and in 8 or 9 big long strides disappeared over the ridge. I didn't tell anyone till I told my father 3 years ago. He confirmed he had seen it before. I'm no longer sure it's in the area. I've gone out and have attempted to see him since with no luck.

Second time was in 2005. I was at a popular swim hole near the Jenkinsburg bridge. It could have been a bear but I have never seen a bear push over a 30 foot tall pine tree. It was a glimpse and then I saw the tree fall forcefully and looked back and whatever it was, was gone.

Both the 3rd and 4th encounter happened in the same night, at the same location, in March of this year. Me and my current girlfriend went down to do some night fishing. The first encounter of the night was of one I wanna say was stalking us on the high trail leading into the fishing spot. He followed us for a solid 15 minutes and disappeared when I caught sight of him in the moonlight. We finished fishing around 1 am and we went back to the car in the gravel parking lot. We then heard several guttural howls along with 2 distinct wood knocks. As we started to walk towards the car we had several 6 inch diameter stones thrown at us. Mind you we were THE ONLY PEOPLE THERE.

Encounter in Monongalia County, 1978

Sent in by a WV C.A.S.E follower who would like to remain anonymous.
Date: Late June, early July 1978
Time of year: Summer
Location: Near the WV-PA border in Monongalia County near
   Blacksville, WV
Nearest road: Tom's Run
Nearest town: Brave, PA
Nearest water source: Dunkard Creek

Eyewitness description:
What I saw was a very large bipedal animal with long, heavy reddish
brown hair.

Here's my Bigfoot encounter: (I reported it to Stan Gordon a few years
ago, too). When I was about 11 years old, I was playing in the woods near
my house, beside an abandoned house that was falling in. My mother had
forbade me to go there but my friend Susie and I did quite a few times.
Susie got somewhat ahead of me while I was distracted by this old house.
An interior wall was exposed and there was an old calendar visible. I was
trying to get a good look without going "in" but realized Susie wasn't right
there. I turned to run after her and literally bumped into it. At age 11, I
would guess I wasn't quite 5 feet tall and I hit right about the abdomen
of this creature. He was covered in long, heavy reddish brown hair. I
took a quick glance up and immediately ran as fast as my chubby legs
would carry me. While I was running I began to think it was probably
my brothers or their friends pulling some kind of joke on me but I soon
found out differently. I came out of the woods behind a neighbor's house
about five houses away from my house. In their pool in the backyard were
both of my brothers and their friends swimming. There was no way they
could've beaten me and me not have seen them. As for Susie, when I

found her she had made it home but swears to this day she never saw a thing. I don't remember a smell, or how it looked in the face but guess it was at least 7ft tall. I am now 51 and will never forget it.

Additional Information
I grew up in Brave, PA, and the West Virginia border runs a few hundred feet away from the house I grew up in. At the point I was in the woods might have been considered West Virginia.

Question: I'm just asking this question because I'm sure someone else probably will. Could it have been someone that was staying in the abandoned house? Like a homeless person?
Answer: No. There was no roof and the exterior wall had collapsed. Us kids happened upon it while we were out and mentioned it to our parents who told us to stay away, that there might be an old well or other dangerous things there. The town historian at the time was well into his 80s and said that place had been abandoned since he was a "young man." I truly believe what I encountered was Bigfoot. I still live in Brave. My brother lives a few miles up the road and my daughter (in her 20s), my husband and I were there at dark a while about a year ago and we all swear we heard "whoops" in the woods behind his place.

Question: Do you believe that there could be one still in the area?
Answer: Yes, I do. For what it's worth, I've always had the sense that the Bigfoot are connected to the Native Americans and this area has a lot of Native American history.

Question: Is the area you had your encounter still accessible?
Answer: It's so grown up that I believe you'd need a four wheeler to get to it. Years ago there was an old grown up access road but I don't know if you could even discern where the road was. I can point to the area from the road below where I currently live.

Screams in Mingo County

Thanks to WV C.A.S.E follower Mr. Todd Browning for sending in this awesome story of an experience he had in Gilbert, Mingo County.

County: Mingo County
Time Of Year: October

Source of the screams?
Mr. O'Dell, it was one October morning. I remember it was early season and I had been hunting my regular place. This particular morning, I decided not to ride my Can-Am to the spot, but park it short of my stand. I was about 150 yards from the stand. It was an hour and a half before daybreak. I climbed a small incline to the old logging road and started walking. It was hot that morning and I was extremely overdressed. I stopped to cool down and catch my breath. I can assure you that I am familiar with the animals in my woods, and how they sound, and how they move through leaves. I have hunted for at least 40 years.

While I was waiting for my breath to catch me, I was looking eastward and could barely see the rays coming over the mountain. That's when I heard it. A scream like no other I had ever heard and about 50 to 80 yards behind and above me on a point. I turned around startled and the hair on my head stood up. Hard to do as I have none. LOL. About ten seconds or so, I heard an answer. This came from across the valley on the point directly opposite me, distinctly two different critters. It wasn't daybreak yet and I was sooo upset that I nocked an arrow, hoping I wouldn't have to use it. I don't know why, but to me it sounded as if they were alarmed. They knew I was there. I started on in a few minutes thinking, oh well, whatever. Then the one closest to my position, screamed again and this time, immediately, the other one across the valley answered back. It was then that I heard something break a small branch as if it stepped on it.

Then leaves rustling. I'm not sure if that was an animal that got nervous and ran or that thing making the noise.

By this time, I wasn't worried how hot it was. I just wanted to get to my stand. So much for sneaking in and not disturbing anything. While I was on my way, the sounds never got closer but were in the same place. About 5 times they answered one another. I got in my stand and nothing unusual happened for the rest of the hunt. I sat that day until 11 or so. I did think it was odd that I never seen so much as a squirrel that day. I have never heard it since or captured anything on trail cam. I do know this. I have hunted ever since I was old enough to walk with my grandad. I have never heard anything like that, ever.

Vocalizations in Morgan County

Sent in by Michael Shongo.
Year: 2002-2003
County: Morgan
Nearest town: Omps
Nearest water source: Small creek (name unknown)

Question: Do think you have encountered Bigfoot?
Answer: Yes, I do believe I did. Nothing dangerous, but yes. I have a friend that owns some property in West Virginia about 2 miles east of Cacapon State Park off of Route 522. In 2002 or 2003, I was staying at his place in the summer. I went there a lot back then. I never saw any animals there, not so much as a chipmunk. There was a 1970s trailer there and a makeshift tree fort about 150 feet or so behind the trailer in the woods with what seemed to be patted down growth under it.

One Saturday, some good ole boys using a bulldozer were bringing in a trailer nearly identical to the one I stayed at, to a piece of property on the other side of the power lines. Between the properties are huge power lines and 100 feet or so of clear field between us. Around dusk I heard two deep throated howls I will never forget.

I have been back on the property many times since. The atmosphere has changed. There are a family of ground hogs living in the log piles now. I've seen birds and chipmunks. At the time this happened no one lived within that area. The dirt road is now gravel and two families live back there. After my friend gave them the trailer he had, he now has a fifth wheel mobile. A few times I heard something large moving around the trailer. Once I thought the new trailer was nudged.

Sighting in Nicholas County, 2018

Type Of Sighting: Road Crossing
Year: 2018, November
County: Nicholas
Nearest Town: Drennen
Nearest Road: Route 39
Nearest Waterway: Peters Creek

Description Of What You Saw:
8-10 feet tall, very hairy, muscular, wet, black, matted dirty hair. Legs looked same size from ankle to hip. Not a bear. Arms seemed to hang to knees.

Your Story:
While driving on a rainy November night around 8:00pm, our lights shone on something along the right side of Route 39. Near Route 39 we came to a stop as this thing walked on all fours to the center of the road and stood up on two legs. It stood there for a short period and then walked off the left side of the road. After walking along the edge of the road for a short distance before dropping on all fours again and climbing the hill. We then lost sight of it. It was not a bear.

Male witness:
I'm 63 years old and have spent most of my life hunting these woods and never seen anything or even believed something like this could exist. But I do now. I know what I saw and no one can change that.

West Virginia Cryptids and Strange Encounters co-founder Justin and I went to Nicholas County to talk to a couple that claimed to have had

a Bigfoot sighting in November of 2018 near the town of Drennen. We took a report along with a drawing done by the female witness.
We also took several pictures where the sighting took place and measured distances from where they first seen it and when it finally crossed the road.

The witnesses also picked out a picture of a face from several pictures we use to obtain not only a description but a reaction from the witnesses. Both witnesses picked the same face photo. (photos are artist renderings of other witness descriptions) The following pictures are of the sighting area, report, drawing, and face photo they picked.

Drawing by the female witness in Nicholas County.

Artist rendering chosen by both witnesses.
On top of drawing for comparison.

Sighting in Nicholas County, 2015

Sent in by a WV C.A.S.E follower who would like to remain anonymous.
County: Nicholas County
Date: November 2015

Shared Account:
On Nov. 24th, 2015, I was hunting deer during firearm season back on the hill behind my house. I am going bonkers for lack of a better word, trying to process what I saw that day. I was walking up an old dirt road. The ground was wet, leaves etc. so I was very quiet. I reached an area where I was looking down into the forest. I raised up my binoculars because I, at that moment, was expecting to see a smaller black bear. As I was looking at its back I noticed a very thin white hair line running down the middle of its back. I thought that's a strange marking for a black bear. I continued watching this creature, for quite a few minutes. I wanted to see its face. Slowly it turned its head and it was as if it were looking into my eyes through the binoculars. Its face was solid black of the blackest night, very shiny, looked almost like black leather stretched tight. Its nose was very wide and had huge nostrils. It seemed to be hunkered down by an old fallen tree and it was in the sunshine that was beaming through parts the forest. It had no hair on its face. Everything was black. Its face looked human. I could see ears like mine, only black. Its hair on its body was a lighter black than its face and somewhat thin compared to a black bear's. And it wasn't dirty or mangled - it looked clean.

In the meantime, as I was steadily watching it, small sandstone rocks were coming down by me from the road above. I didn't want to turn and look. I was watching the creature below me and figured it was chipmunks running around behind me causing small rocks to fall but after seeing that face I had to look. I saw nothing behind me. When I returned to using the binoculars and looking for it, it was gone. No sound whatsoever.

I now feel that something behind me was trying to get my attention so it could get away.

Someone said that it was probably a man in one of those strange looking suits to hunt in. My reply was, he needs to get mental help immediately for the fact that everyone on this mountain this week are carrying high powered rifles. (I never once felt scared or threatened, all was calm.) I saw no limbs, arms, legs - I was focused on its head. It wasn't huge like the width of it. As I stated before, from behind it looked like a small bear (except it had a human like face).

Sighting in Nicholas County, 2010

Nearest town: Richwood
Nearest water source: North Fork of the Cherry River
Nearest road: Rt. 39/55 between Richwood and Marlinton. As you're leaving Richwood, it is between the first and second bridge that crosses the river.
Month: August 2010
Time off day: Late, around 10 or 11 p.m.

Witness description:
Color: dark fur. Height: taller than 5'9, much bigger than me. Size: broad shoulders, definitely at least 200 pounds by my best guess. Facial features: I did not see the face, as it went behind me from left to right. I turned toward the sound and there it was going across the yard. Bi-ped and running with a large stride.

I used to think people who talked about this were "certified crazy" until I saw one myself in August of 2010 in Nicholas County. It definitely was NOT a bear. It was dark, but there was enough light coming off of the porch at my cabin to get a good glimpse of it. I was out in the yard on a lawn chair looking at the stars. I heard something in the woods behind me. Thinking it was a bear, I decided I would go ahead and get back in the house. As I approached the porch, it ran across the yard and was only about 10 feet from me. It was moving on two feet and was taller than me. I'm 5'10. It ran over the bank and across the river, and I assume across the road and on up the mountain on the other side. I have a very docile Labrador retriever, and I've never seen her react like she did that night. She came off of the porch barking and growling after it and stopped at the river bank. It left a stench that was a mix of musty and dead animal.

Additional witness comment:
I didn't stay at the cabin by myself for a long while, but I am able to now.

Sightings Near Nicholas-Greenbrier County Line

Here is an awesome account about three Bigfoot sightings sent in by WV C.A.S.E follower Jeffery L. Bennett.

Eyewitness Account:
I seen 3 Bigfoots at different times near the Nicholas-Greenbrier County line. One was really big and gray colored. The other two looked black or dark colored and they were different sizes. I seen them different days over about a 3-4 month period. The gray one I seen about daybreak. One of the others was at night and the other early evening. I was going up the backroad between Fenwick and Rupert over Beech Knob. The sightings took place in summer and one in late fall.

I've always believed in them. This just confirmed it. I'm a hunter so I know it wasn't a bear like most people say and I just pay a little more attention now hoping to see more. Really it was scary but like I said, I just pay more attention now.

Sighting in Preston County, 2014

Date: October 5, 2014
Location: Near Bruceton Mills
County: Preston

Eyewitness Account:
My fiancé B. and I just got done watching a movie, when the dogs started barking. Then within 5 minutes they got really quiet and went into their dog houses. We thought this was strange, so we opened our back door toward where the dogs were barking at a few minutes before and saw something near our mineral feeder for the cows. We live on a farm, so we had an unused mineral feeder in the back yard.

It looked at first that it was on all 4 legs, and as big as the outline was, we assumed it was a bear, until it stood up on two legs. Now mind you we still thought it was a bear because, well you know bears do stand on their hind legs. We had our back porch light on so we could see it, but the thing we saw was still about maybe 80 feet away. Anyway, what we thought was strange was after it stood up it heard us at our back door and turned its head our way. And when it did we saw big yellow like eyes. We looked at each other to make sure we were both seeing the same thing. Then we saw its side arm move and it looked like it was below its knees. When it started to walk away it walked mostly upright on 2 legs swinging its arms and still looking at us until it turned its head to the hay field and walked away. To this day we still can't explain what we saw, but we did see it.

Sighting in Ritchie County, 1974

Sent in by WV C.A.S.E follower Timothy Grogg. His sighting took place in 1974 when he was a young boy in Smithville.
Date Of Sighting: 1974
Location: Smithville
County: Ritchie

Shared Account:
Most people do not believe in Bigfoot. I do believe in Bigfoot, because in 1974 I saw him. My older sister Becky does also. I will start with some background info. When we were kids, my Grandma and Grandpa Wells lived in a God forsaken hollow just outside the town of Smithville, West Virginia. This is one of the spookiest houses I have ever been in. In the daytime it was great. It had a huge yard and lots of places that kids could play.

My family went down one weekend to visit and stay overnight. My uncle Hatzel (mom's brother), his wife and kids were in to visit also. Grandpa always had 4 or 5 dogs on the place to keep varmints away. Uncle Hartzel had brought his dog, which was a big Norwegian Elkhound cross breed named Nikki. This dog was tough. He was turned loose to roam the farm. He bullied and whipped every dog on the place. He was king of the dog world and was afraid of nothing. (Now remember this because it will come up later in the story.)

We had a good time playing with our cousins and just roaming around the yard. When night came on, all the kids were brought inside. All of the adults, other than my grandparents were drinking beer and visiting. Now remember this house had no running water and no indoor bathroom. The women would go outside on the porch and pee in a coffee can to keep from going all the way to the out-house. It was getting late, probably around 11:00 pm. The adults were getting ready to get us and them into bed.

All of a sudden, every dog on the place started barking their heads off. Grandpa started yelling at them to shut up, but they wouldn't stop. Then they all stop at once. My aunt Thelma and sister Becky are out on the back porch doing their business before bed. All at once the "big bad" Nikki comes around the house whimpering, with his tail tucked between his legs. My sister asked Thelma what was wrong with Nikki. Thelma replied that whatever scared that dog must be bad. She got herself and Becky back in the house and told the men.

Hatzel said that if Nikki was afraid of something, we had big problems. My dad, who was on crutches, and Hartzel (aka Hooter) went out on the porch. Hartzel and dad saw something and Hartzel fumbled around and fell off the porch.

I can remember my dad yelling, "Hooter, it's coming!" And he threw one of his crutches at it. They came back inside with scared looks on their faces. I was old enough to stand at the window and pull myself up to see. I saw this image go through the yard, walking on two legs, just as they came in the door. The dogs never barked at this time and Nikki went under the porch and stayed till morning. The adults locked the doors, and no one got much sleep that night. We went out the next morning and got dad's crutch. The ground was so dry that there were no tracks.

I can still see that image of something walking in my mind. It was walking too fast to be a bear. I can't explain it and for some reason there was never anything said about it after that. My sister and I still to this day talk about it. No one believes us, but I know what I saw. I believe it was Bigfoot!

Sighting at Bluestone Lake, 2016

Shared by Alfon Cani Cook
Date: 2016
Location: Bluestone Lake

Eyewitness Account:
I seen something at Bluestone lake 2 years ago. I was on the lake fishing and when I popped around a point something with black shining hair was kneeling down. When it seen me it jumped up and ran up the hill on two feet. You could hear it breaking tree limbs and stomping up the hill. In just a minute or so a deer come running out of the woods, jumped in the water and came out almost to my boat. I have never seen a deer act like that one did. What I saw was not a bear. I've seen plenty of bears and bears don't run on two feet hopefully. It could have only been one thing. Bigfoot.

Sighting in Summers County, 30 years ago

County: Summers
Date: 30 years ago
Time Of Year: late December

Eyewitness Account of Tom Hopkins:
I seen something about 30 years ago while bow hunting on Indian Mills near Bluestone Lake. I was 15 at the time and it was in late December near the end of bow season at around 9 a.m. and I was in a ground blind on a ridge. I first thought it was a bear heading my way walking down the ridge line and I got a bit excited but noticed it was on two feet as it got closer. It then stopped about 100 yards away at a tree and appeared to sit down at the base of the tree and I thought it was another hunter. I then started thinking there weren't a lot of folks hunting that late in the season, just me and my uncle on that day. So I thought that was odd. It appeared to be dark brown and I couldn't make out any features or color variations. It then got up and started circling the tree on two legs at first and then would squat down for a bit and then would circle around some more on two feet and kind of a duck walk. This went on for about 10 minutes. I was getting a little nervous because it just didn't seem normal. I was getting a gut feeling that this thing wasn't a human, and I might have to shoot this thing if it comes my way, and all I had was a bow. Then after that it just went back the same direction it had came from, until it went out of sight. I still remember it to this day.

WV C.A.S.E: Question: Wow. Could you make out how big it was?
Answer, Tom Hopkins: It was fairly large but couldn't really tell. It was at least 100 yards away and through brush and trees. If it would have been late spring or summer, I wouldn't have even seen it for the leaves.
I have heard of a lot of sightings near the Hinton and Bluestone area. There is a visitors center at Sandstone right off the interstate. I have heard

stories of families of Bigfoot type creatures being spotted walking near there. I asked a park ranger there last summer if he had heard these stories and he said yes but had never seen anything himself.

WV C.A.S.E Question: Did it have a humanoid shape?
Answer, Tom Hopkins: Yes, and it moved like a person. Transitioning smoothly from the ground to its feet. I have seen black bears in the woods before and it didn't move like a bear.

WV C.A.S.E: Did you notice anything strange before you saw the creature?
Answer, Tom Hopkins: No. The movement first caught my attention. No sound or smell. Didn't run or move fast at all.

WV C.A.S.E Question: Are you comfortable saying what you saw was possibly a Bigfoot?
Answer, Tom Hopkins: I have never seen anything like that since. It was something strange and it freaked me out and still to this day I remember it. I would say it is a strong possibility.

Encounter in Upshur County, 2017

A very interesting possible Sasquatch encounter sent by WV C.A.S.E follower Anthony Crislip.
County: Upshur
Date: October 13, 2017

Witness Account:
Okay, here is my possible encounter. Approximately the weekend of October 13th, 2017, my neighborhood childhood friends and I went camping at Beans Mill in Upshur County. I took Friday off to secure a site in case of a crowded weekend. I made it there by 7:30 a.m. After setting up camp around 10:30 a.m., I noticed a strong musky smell that resembles a wet coyote den with a faint skunk type mixed in. It came out of nowhere and lasted until noon or so. I thought nothing of it really.

Then around two o'clock I heard what I thought were several people walking down the road talking, but the strange thing is I never saw anyone walk and the road was in sight. I could clearly hear but couldn't make out the conversation and it also sounded off in some way. I couldn't put my finger on it. I heard at least three distinct voices - just couldn't make out what was said. The weird thing is I had a clear view of the road frontage for about sixty yards long and I was probably that far away, and I thought why would they be walking through the mountain laurel and not the road. But I didn't give it much thought at the time. This lasted about five minutes. So about thirty minutes after that the smell returned for about an hour and a half, then was gone again.

Then shortly after that a small rock about the size of a golf ball, maybe smaller, came down through the canopy about ten yards from where I was sitting. Needless to say, I got a little nervous. I had a side arm and shotgun with me, so I figured I was O.K. After walking around camp and the outskirts I shrugged it off and turned the radio on and waited for my friends to show up. By six o'clock everyone was there, and we had nothing happen that night.

Saturday was eventless until around ten thirty at night. We had movement on our outskirts with small branch breaks and possible heavy footsteps. We all were armed very, very well, and walked the outskirts for about twenty minutes. We had possible eye shine about ten feet off the ground and forty yards away briefly. After that the rest of the night was calm and peaceful, except for all the snoring.

Oh, and one more thing. We checked the whole area that weekend and there were no other campers, and we only saw one vehicle drive up the road.

Sighting in Wyoming County, 7 years ago

Sent in by WV C.A.S.E follower Geneva Worley.
County: Wyoming
Date: 7 years ago

Eyewitness Account:
So this is my Bigfoot story. We were living in Wyoming county in the little town of Ravencliff. We went to Oceana to eat. It was dark when we headed home. We came into Glen Fork. In one section of the town there is not a lot around except a little compression station for a gas well that sets down over the hill from the main road. The embankment going down to the compressor is steep and there is a guardrail along the road. My husband was driving and he had the high beams on. When we got to the guardrail it pulled itself up over the guardrail rail. My husband swerved. I screamed. I looked it dead in the face and could see it really good because of the bright lights. Its face was very dark, flat forehead, not much of a nose, protruding chin. Shaggy thick hair, brown, almost black completely around the face, very long and big arms covered in hair. My husband turned around at the next wide spot but nothing was there by then. We went back the next day and pulled down the little gravel road going to the compressor. The backside this creature came up over was a good 5 foot above my head. (I stand 5'6) It came up it like it was nothing. It completely blew my mind.

Encounter in Webster County

A possible Bigfoot encounter sent in by a WV C.A.S.E follower who is an author that I've gotten to know thru her work. She has been working on a book about West Virginia monsters and had the experience while doing so.

County: Webster

Location: outside of Camden County Route 7/6

Witness Account:

So I'm on a trip this week getting the last pics for the book and I was driving outside Camden, County Route 7/6, Camden-On-Gauley, West Virginia, on Gauley near Cranberry Glades. It was near a place someone had seen a Bigfoot and called Yahoo Holler.

I'd stopped at a church to take some pics and not expecting anything, in a hurry to finish. Broad daylight. As I drove up the road slowly to take some more pics, I heard a knock-knock. I slowed the jeep more to take more pics when something big dove in the thick brush (not a deer, no snort, too thick for deer) and then another knock-knock and a horrible smell like burnt cabbage and skunk like it emitted it when it saw me getting out. It lingered in the jeep for a half hour. The brush was too thick to explore and probably on private property so I didn't dive in too. Just food for thought. Definitely odd!

Encounter in Wetzel County

County: Wetzel

Eyewitness Account:
This takes place in a relatively secluded section of Wetzel County. I had recently lost my vehicle and my only form of transport was by ATV. I would drive my 4-wheeler out to a friend's taking ridge tops and bike trails, always steering clear of main highways. Well, one night I had stayed at my friend's house a little later than usual, and was heading home around 1 am. If you have ever been on a ridge top on an ATV at night, then you know how dark, isolated and vulnerable you are.

I was already hesitant to drive back so late, compounded by the fact that I had almost emptied the main tank of fuel and might have to switch to the reserve tank to get home. I was riding along the ridge, completely surrounded by trees and foliage, well away from ANY homes or people. I had to stop to check to make sure I had my phone and belongings, and as I was sitting there idling, I heard loud thrashing and movement coming from the hillside above the trail. This alone was not enough to scare me as I just brushed it off as normal wood noises or an animal.

Continuing down the path, I came to a section where the foliage was particularly dense on both side of the trail. I had to slow down a bit to ensure safety, and just as I was passing through the thick of it, a large rock (boulder really), a bit smaller than a woman's basketball came sailing over top of the foliage and had I not hit the brakes rather suddenly it would most likely have struck me on the head and knocked me right off or killed me outright.

Suddenly I was in full fight or flight mode. My mind had barely registered what it had seen before it was telling me to GO. I obliged and hammered down, wanting to at least get off this trail and on to a less isolated road. Well, I made it about a half a mile, to where the trail connected back to a more used road. It was here that the ATV began to sputter, running out of fuel. I HAD to stop, the engine had shut off and I reached over to switch to reserve. Sitting in the dark, only red brake lights on the trail behind and straight ahead lights on the path ahead, pushing the ignition hoping it would start, I was petrified. I heard heavy footfall in the woods on the side of path the rock had come from, could see tree limbs shaking and moving headed my way.

Not my manliest moment, but I will admit that I vomited on the path out of fear. After using choke, the bike fired up and I honestly don't remember driving home. Nothing further happened to me but I NEVER was out that late riding West Virginia ridges alone ever again and if you plan to, walk softly but carry a big stick. Preferably a stick that fires bullets.

Sighting in Wyoming County, 2013/2014

An interesting Bigfoot sighting sent in by WV C.A.S.E follower Patricia Shumate.
County: Wyoming
Location: Itmann
Date: October 5th, 2013/2014

Eyewitness Account:
It was October 5 years ago in Itmann that I saw what at first I thought was a very large bear. I was sitting in the ambulance outside my partner's home waiting for him. I was watching some very large birds in the tree tops on the ridge of a cliff across the river.

I had seen what seemed to be a broken tree trunk but did not pay it much attention until the "tree trunk" stood up. At first I thought, "cool, it's a bear."Then I noticed how long its arms were. They were well past its hips. It was dark brown or black. It was far enough away that I was not scared. It stood there for a few seconds. Its back was towards me, then it turned profile and there were NO bear features. I could have seen a muzzle, the face looked kinda flat. It walked away over the mountain in long human like steps. From where I was it looked over 7 foot tall, and yea I know how tall that is (had a partner one time that was 7 feet). I now watch the ridge line and woods all the time in hopes of seeing another one, knowing I was blessed to see this one. I truly believe God put them here for a purpose, and only time will tell what that is. This thing looked too human like - have since heard others tell of seeing this creature while hunting on Bud mountain and that they ran or just did not say anything in fear of being call crazy. Well, folks can call me crazy all they want. I know what I saw that day and consider myself lucky to have seen it.

The Polk Gap Monster, 1992

An encounter shared by WV C.A.S.E follower Dave Paul Lane of a creature that has become known as the "Polk Gap Monster"
County: Wyoming
Location: Pineville
Date: 1992, Summer

Eyewitness Account:
My sighting in Wyoming County. It was the summer of 1992. Myself and my friend Jimmy Perdue were traveling late one night to Pineville. As we were near the bottom of Saulsville mountain on the Pineville side my peripheral vision caught a glimpse on the right hand side of the mountain - a large human like figure covered in very light gray hair was climbing up near the top of the mountain that had been cut for the road way. We both noticed the figure and at the bottom of the mountain we pulled off into a wide spot so we could turn around. While we were trying to turn another vehicle was approaching. The vehicle was traveling at a normal rate of speed as it went by us and disappeared around the curve going up the mountain. We got back on the highway and saw as we rounded the curve, the car that just passed us was stopped in the roadway. The car motioned us around using its blinker. We pulled up to the side of the car and the driver's window was down. The only thing that the driver said was, "did you see that too?" The driver was female and the passenger was male. Jimmy and I were both teenagers and the other drivers appeared to be in there 30 to 40 age range. I regret not getting their names that night.

Jimmy and I could not come up with a plausible explanation of what we saw. What I was sure of is that it appeared large, human like, and covered in grey fur. We could make out that the figure was climbing using its arms and legs to reach the top of the small high-wall next to the road. We decided not to talk about the sighting. We knew that people would think that we were lying or they would come up with another explanation of what we saw.

Now, fast forward about 12 years from that sighting. One of my best friends had bought an Exxon gas station not far from where Jimmy and I had the sighting. He had allowed David "Bugs" Stover, a local retired schoolteacher, local historian, park naturalist, and beloved story teller to sell some books that he wrote at his store in Saulsville. One day I stopped in there and saw a book on the counter and purchased it. The book was a collection of Wyoming County legends of strange sightings, ghost stories, and one that caught my attention was "The Polk Gap Monster." Who hasn't heard stories about BigFoot? But this story was different. It told the tale of a grey fur covered human like figure. Since then, all of the sightings I've heard of about the Polk Gap Monster talk of grey fur, just like what Jimmy and I saw. I found Bugs and told him of our sighting many years prior to him writing the book.

I know there is skepticism and rightly so, but I know what I saw climbing the hillside on a dark summer's night. It wasn't human and it wasn't small. Everything about it said Bigfoot except for the grey fur.

I'll never forget that sighting as long as I live and thankfully I know now that other people throughout the years have seen a similar creature in that area. So, if you're ever in the Twin Falls and McGraws areas of Wyoming County, keep your eyes open on the hills and hollers. I do and always will.

Sighting in Wyoming County, 2013/2014

A possible Bigfoot sighting sent in by WV C.A.S.E follower Brian
Martin.
Town: Wyoming
County: Wyoming
Date: Winter of 2013/2014
Nearest Rd: Rt. 97
Nearest water source: Guyandotte River

Subject Description:
It was very dark colored, almost black looking. Couldn't tell for sure about
hair but it was between 8 and 10 feet tall. I am 6' 2 and it was way taller
than me.

I was driving a dump truck on night shift during the winter of 2013/2014.
I was coming through the small town of Wyoming in Wyoming County
between 2 and 3 in the morning. About 50 feet from the road, I saw what
I first thought was a man. I thought it was strange that he would be there
at that time of the night in the winter. It was just barely lit by a street
light that was a pretty good way from it. As I got closer, I realized it was
way too tall to be a man. It was standing in the open where someone had
thrown out some bags of trash or something, so I figured it was looking
for food maybe. It just stood there as I drove by and never moved.

I went through there the next day to make sure it wasn't a mannequin
or something and it was gone. I live close to there and drive that road a
lot. I have never seen anything standing in that area before or after that
night. It was an awesome experience and one I will never forget. I was
already a believer, but it did make my heart jump. I have since been a lot
more aware that there are things in this world that we just don't have all

the answers for. I have also heard some strange calls and wood knocks near Baileysville.

Sighting in Wyoming County, 1974

Provided by WV C.A.S.E follower Topher Adkins.
Year:1974
Time of year: Fall
Nearest Town: Otsego
County: Wyoming
Nearest water source: pond

Eyewitness:
When I was about 7 years old, Dad and I saw one at top of Otsego Holler on strip road by a big pond. On edge of water squatting down and it quickly stood up and turned and disappeared into the woods of hemlock pines.

That day changed my life. Dad grabbed me up and down the hill to the truck and he got us away as fast as he could. It looked at me from the other side of the pond as we came up over the hill. Dad was 6'3 and about 250 pounds. It made him look small.

Dark brown to black hair and where sun hit it was kinda orange on ends of fur. Was too far to see face, but when we popped over lower ridge of bank it was squatting right at water by bushes. It heard us, stood up, turned on a dime and in 2 steps was vanished into the hemlock pines. It had to have a huge stride to go that far with two steps. Dad got me in the truck and down the mountain and said not to ever mention what we saw. He called it the Protector of the Woods. He said leave him be. It must have been 1974 cause my sister was 2 at the time.

We were in an old green Ford pickup truck with silver chrome and white. Green seats and dash. Wow, I remember more than I thought. It was cold and we had gone up to cut firewood and my job was to throw into the truck. No wood that day!

WV C.A.S.E Question: Was there a reason why your dad called it the Protector of the Woods?
Witness Answer: Dad was half Cherokee on his Mom's side. Dad's full Cherokee grandmother told me of the Peace Keepers of the wood. Ma Sparks told me about how when she was little in winter they were snowed in and starving. She said the Peace Keepers brought a fresh kill deer and left on edge of the yard line on the mountain. She said they saved them.

She never had cows but she always kept a block of salt block by the edge of her yard. She said they liked it. It was looking out for each other. She said you knew when they were around from a sweet death smell that would be in the air. She bragged that she never lost any chickens or other animals because of their agreement. Wish I could go back and ask better questions.

Vocalizations in Wyoming County, 2016

Encounter sent in by a WV C.A.S.E follower who would like to remain anonymous.
Year: June 2016
Time: 4 a.m.
Nearest road: Rt. 97
Nearest town: Baileysville
Nearest water source: Horse Creek Lake

Witness Account:
It was 2016, around early June, because school just let out. Me and a few buddies were catfishing at Horse Creek Lake at about 4 a.m. We started to hear some brush being broke, but we brushed it off as maybe being deer. It was just about daylight when we heard the hollers start. They were going back and forth to each other. We left the lake and drove up the road that leads to Hanover about a mile or two from the trash compactor in Baileysville. We got about three hundred feet up the road and stopped, turned the truck off and just listened. We heard it again about 5 minutes later. With a spotlight we started scanning the brush and old logging roads to see if we could see anything. But nothing was there.

Encounter in Berkeley County

An interesting story shared by WV C.A.S.E follower Brad Arvin.
Location: East of Martinsburg
County: Berkeley
Nearest Water: Opequon Creek

Witness Account:
Back when I was 7 or 8 years old, I always tagged along with my Grand Pap and Uncle to check the trap line they had set. My Pap trapped foxes, raccoons, opossum, skunks, and muskrats to supplement his income. He used the dual spring leg traps to do this. We butchered a lot of hogs and used the lungs as bait that we hung over the traps to bring in the animals.

One morning we discovered 4 maybe 5 of those traps completely torn apart! All in a line on this game trail. They were spaced about 25 or so yards apart. After discovering the first 3, my Pap and Uncle had a discussion that they left me out of. I seen concern on their faces but at my age I didn't know what to think. I asked what did it and they told me that a bobcat had done it. At that age I believed it. But, looking back I remember that they started carrying the .44 Mag along with a 12 gauge shotgun and a .22 to dispatch the animals in the traps. After that season they never trapped that area again.

Many years later I deer hunted that property. I had rocks the size of softballs thrown at me and a friend while we were standing on a deer drive. There's several other things that I experienced over the years on this property as well. It's a large tract of land to the east of Martinsburg. It borders the Opequon Creek. It runs South all the way to the CSX Rail Line. My guess is that something got its hand (paw) in those traps and pulled them completely apart. Bigfoot? Maybe. I know now a bobcat isn't capable of doing that.

I just wish my Pap and Uncle were still alive to verify it. I will say this. It's no coincidence that Bigfoot became a topic in our home after this occurred. We watched everything we could back then on the subject, and it never dawned on me why till much, much later. It all made sense then. They were hiding the truth from me because I was only 7 or 8 at the time - didn't wanna scare me.

Cubey Wiley's Monster, 1960s

County: Raleigh
Location: Naoma Area
Time: 1960s

Shared Account:
Raleigh County is said to be home to many animals that roam its woods, such as black bears, wild hogs and even mountain lions. But did you know that a man by the name of Cubey Wiley in the late 1960s claimed that a monster of some sort also roamed the same woods around the Naoma area of Raleigh County?

He spoke of hearing a loud screaming coming from the nearby woods and in his words, "Sounded like a big elephant." Some say that it was another local named Woody Boogs just blowing through a large car horn to prank ole Cubey. Others say it was the scream of a mountain lion or possibly Bigfoot.

We may never know what Cubey was hearing, but it is said that many heard the mysterious sound and many claim to still hear it to this day. One person is quoted as saying, "It sounded awful, almost human." Another said, "I heard it the other night and was shocked. It sounded almost like it was in the wind, it kinda traveled by. I was on the back porch which is about 100 feet from the edge of the woods. I almost fell getting back into the house."

Could it be a mountain lion, a Bigfoot type creature, or is it just some prankster walking the bush with an old car horn? We may never know.

Sighting in Monroe County, 11 years ago

County: Monroe
Location: Near Indian Creek and New River
Time 11 years Ago, Mid-August

Eyewitness Account:
I was 22 at the time. I was driving to the river with some friends in mid-August at night. The truck I was driving had 33 inch tires and a lift kit so it set up higher than most. About a quarter mile down the gravel road I noticed movement out of the corner of my eye up on the hill to my left, about 1/2 mile from the river. It came down in front of the truck. I about hit it! I had to slam on the brakes. It just turned toward us for a brief moment. It seemed like it was just as spooked as we were. Then it kept going across the gravel road and down the other side of the hill.

Its hair was a grayish color and it had a lot of it. It was very big. It had to be at least 7 foot tall. Also, it didn't have a neck. Very long arms and legs. Its thumbs wasn't like ours. I'm positive it was a Bigfoot!

Sighting in Tucker County, 2008

County: Tucker County
Location: Canaan Valley National Wildlife Refuge
Date: 2008

Eyewitness Account:
I was hunting West Virginia's late antler-less deer season in the Canaan Valley National Wildlife Refuge when the sighting occurred. I had gotten to the area shortly after 3:00 p.m. that evening, and after parking my vehicle in the Camp 70 parking area, I hiked up what appeared to be an old logging trail directly behind the parking area.

I had already gotten a late start and wanted to get afield as quickly as possible, so I decided to stalk along the logging trail until I got further into the river bottom. After hunting the trail for roughly 30 minutes I was able to see a long distance in the river bottom to my right, so I decided to move into the bottom in hopes a deer would emerge from the thick along the river at dusk. I came across another road after leaving the logging trail, so I started walking further into the valley on it. The road was frozen and crusted over due to the cold temperatures, which made traveling quietly impossible. So after a short distance I found a small group of trees a few yards from the trail and set up in them.

Shortly after arriving I heard what sounded like brush breaking 150-200 yards below me, towards the river. I readied myself in hopes it was a group of deer moving into the flats to feed, but nothing appeared. A few minutes passed by and I heard the sound again, and again, but nothing materialized. I decided to move closer, and positioned myself in another group of small trees 100 yards or so below my first site. I had been in this grove of saplings for 5 - 10 minutes when I caught movement in a cluster of trees that was about 80-90 yards below me and to the left.

I could see the movement with my naked eye, and immediately upon seeing it I scoped the group of trees and to my surprise saw nothing. A few minutes went by and I caught the movement again. I quickly scoped the trees, and this time I was shocked by what I saw. At first I thought it was a large man, as the first thing I saw through my scope was a vague silhouette, but when my eyes focused I could see what appeared to be a primate-like creature standing upright and staring directly at me. It only broke its stillness to slightly move the upper portion of its body in an up and down motion. It would bend its knees as if it was going to sit down, then immediately straighten back up. This went on for what seemed to have been over a minute, then the creature exited the group of trees and moved to my left (the creature's right), towards the mountain behind me. It walked across an expanse of river basin that I would guess to be 70-80 yards long before entering the timber and exiting my field of view. It kept watching me the whole time it was walking, only breaking its stare on me a few times to look directly ahead of it. I initially thought of attempting to locate its tracks, but my nerves got the best of me and I started moving towards the parking lot as quickly as I could. Though the creature never actually made any threatening movements, I didn't feel safe enough to continue hunting and remain in the valley any longer after the sun went down than I had to. I immediately left the area and had no further incidents on the way to my vehicle.

Sighting in Braxton County, 1976

County: Braxton
Date: August 17, 1976
Location: Off Interstate 79
Closest Water: Sin Creek

Eyewitness Account:
Ronald Stark and Clifford Barnes drove off Interstate 79 at Skin Creek onto a road to Weston Drive-in Theatre just as it was getting dark. They encountered an apelike thing on road, huge, black, crouched. It straightened up eight feet tall. Stayed in the middle of the road watching them about 30 seconds, then waddled off into the woods. Sheriff's Department was called.

John Fuhrmann reported to John Green. The report was subsequently published in the December 1976 Gray Barker Article.

Sighting in Wyoming County, 1997

Location: Matheny
County: Wyoming
Date: August 1997

Eyewitness Account:
I wasn't sure if it was worth mentioning. I'm still not, but my husband wanted me to tell you. It was in Matheny, West Virginia, in August of 1997. Matheny is a small residential area with wooded hills on all sides and a creek with a concrete bridge crossing it. It was a clear night at around 11:30 p.m. I was sitting alone on the front porch of my uncle's house, which sits on a hill overlooking the area, talking on the phone with my now husband. I noticed that all of the dogs in the area seemed to be barking instead of the usual one or two. I've been around dogs my whole life and these dogs sounded scared.

Anyway, there was a streetlight that allowed part of the neighbor's yard to be seen. I saw some movement in the shadows before this person or thing stepped in the light. It was only a few seconds and I only saw it from the waist but it was tall and covered with dark brown hair. It was walking very quickly. It walked back into the shadows and I heard two large splashes in the creek followed by sounds of it walking on the opposite creek bank. I've tried to include all the details I could remember but, if you have any further questions about this, feel free to contact me.

Sighting in Jackson County, 2000

County: Jackson
Date: 2000

Eyewitness Account:
My name is Charles Justin Hall. I have hunted all my life and am a resident currently in West Virginia. The sighting I am about to mention is something that frightens me to talk about to this day. What makes it worse, no one believes me except for my father Chuck Hall. It all started when we were hunting in Jackson County. It was around noon, and we were in tree stands approximately 25 to 30 feet off of the ground. The habitat was sparse woods and heavy thickets. My dad on one side of the hill, me on the other.

I was becoming bored when something began rustling leaves. It was three deer followed by a large humanoid, or that is how I describe it. It was large, probably around 7 feet, hair covered, except for face. Large sunken nose and a reddish brown eye color with yellowish flat teeth, stocky built, and it smelled very badly.

You are probably wondering why I know all these details. Well, the fact of the matter was I put the Golden Eagle scope up on my gun at a distance of around 100 yards and frankly, was about to pull the trigger. Believe you me, I got a very good look.

The thing that stopped me from shooting, though, was that the creature looked sad and non-aggressive. But that wasn't going to stop me. I was scared like hell. It wasn't until I yelled as loud as a I could, "if you are a human stop right there, and take off the mask or I will shoot." The creature just looked at me and kind of growled. I was watching him through the scope the whole time. I was paralyzed with fear. The creature then turned and bolted, running extremely fast for its size over the hill and straight for my dad. When I got down from the stand my dad said he had seen flashes of the creature but never the whole thing. To this day, I know what I saw.

Sighting in Summers County, 2001

County: Summers
Date: February 2001
Location: near Rt. 20, not far from Bluestone Lake
Nearest City: Hinton

Eyewitness Account:
The terrain was very brushy. I was walking down a mountain when I came cross the creature in a creek bed. I would estimate the creature to have been about 7 feet tall and weighing close to 400 or 500 pounds. The arms were very long and swinging with the movement. There wasn't any hair on its face, the skin was a very dark brown. The eyes were small, black, and round. It walked upright with an almost comical gait. It had a slight slouch. What I saw was a large humanoid creature walking like a human being.

When the creature saw me it slowly and calmly walked away. There was no aggression in the animal at all. Its face was quite ape-like but didn't protrude out at the mouth. I was about 30 yards from the creature whenever we saw each other.

Encounters in Tyler County, 1972

County: Tyler
Nearest City: West Union
Date: Summer 1972, afternoon
Closest Water: Middle Island Creek and a small pond at old abandoned farmhouse
Location: Route 18 near Tyler/Doddridge County border

Eyewitness Account:
I was fishing for Bluegill at an old abandoned farmhouse with two friends from my childhood, Rick and Tim Shepherd. As we were leaving to go home, we saw two, for the lack of a better word, creatures. I don't know if these qualify as a Bigfoot but this is what we saw. Two creatures with bright red hair were lying by the edge of the forest tree line, one atop the other as if making love. They were at least 100 yards away but clearly visible due to the contrast of their color against the straw covered broom sage they were laying in. The thing here is that these were not large creatures but rather around 5'6 to 5'10 or so, straight red hair, bodies slightly thicker than a man's and walked upright on two legs.

When they saw us at around the same time we saw them, they stood up, moved quickly into the woods, and disappeared. The amazing thing to me was that they walked upright like a person save that they were kind of stooped over at the shoulders (as if they were leaning over.) The hair of their pelts was long enough to blow in the wind and in color reminded me of an orangutan. We never got to see their faces as the distance was too great and it all happened suddenly.

Before we went up the sloping hill from the pond, we all remembered hearing noises like muted mewling. I really don't know how to explain the sounds. We were kind of shook up and didn't really tell anyone at the time what we had seen because we knew we would be teased. I haven't seen or spoken to the Shepherd boys in years but I'm betting they remember this too. It's kind of hard to forget.

A slightly recessed pond, like a crater, surrounded by a broom sage field all surrounded by woods. An old, abandoned farmhouse was on the sight. It's probably fallen down now but I could take you to the spot. I told 5 or 6 good friends over the years, but no one else. Only that I've always been curious about what we saw. I have no ideas or preconceived ideas. I only know they were something different and unexplainable. I doubt I will ever know what it was I saw.

In the fall of about 1960, while coon hunting with my grandfather and friend named Bill, we had an encounter with what I am now convinced was a Bigfoot. We had left our house, which sat atop a ridge and went down into our hollow. We had planned to go down the creek about a mile to the next hollow, turn right up this hollow, follow it all the way up, and climb the hill back to the top of the ridge. We would then have an easy walk home on a gravel road, which was the main road in the area at that time. We were about three miles from the nearest blacktop road, which was West Virginia Rt. 2 running beside the Ohio River.

All was normal down the first hollow, but when we started up the second, the dogs returned in an agitated state, and began to growl and raise the hair on their backs. They refused to go up the hollow in the lead as they normally hunted. Instead, they stayed close to the light, which was a kerosene lantern that lit a circle only a few feet wide. We also had a two-cell light, used sparingly to conserve batteries, and a six-volt spotlight, which turned out to have a dead battery.

No amount of encouragement from my grandpa could get the dogs to go do the job they had always done so well. Another hundred yards or so up the hollow, they were even more nervous and sniffed the air with long, deep breaths. They stared intently into the darkness in the direction we were moving, and would not get more than a few yards away, all the while growling, acting in a way we had not seen before. Their actions were really beginning to annoy Grandpa and he was trying to let them know his feeling with a verbal assault on them, their ancestors, and their species in general, but they were unfazed and were staying just out of range of the toe of his boot. We were walking single file through briars and brush with Grandpa in the lead, and then me, with Bill bringing up the rear.

When we reached the point where the terrain started getting steep, somewhere from eighty to one hundred yards straight ahead, there came the most bloodcurdling sound I have ever heard. After another forty or so years of life this sound is still very clear in my mind. It began as a deep bellowing roar that went higher in frequency and ended with a very high AHH-EEE EEE- EEE as best I can describe it. It lasted six to seven seconds. The hardest thing is to try to describe the volume other than to say it could have been heard for miles, and I know of no known animal anywhere that can howl, yell, scream, roar, or trumpet that loud. Whatever made this sound had to be huge. It seemed as if my hair stood up and I had a bitter taste in my mouth, I suppose from adrenalin.

We froze in our tracks for a few seconds then instinct or reflex made me turn to run, but Bill was blocking the path. Grandpa, who was hard of hearing, turned and said, "What the hell was that?" He was born less than a mile from this exact spot and had spent his life hunting, trapping, and just walking these hills. He was the best woodsman I ever knew, so if he didn't know what it was, I sure as hell didn't know. It would be several more years before any of us ever heard of Bigfoot. Bill also was a true woodsman, who had gotten game and herbs from these hills all his life. I was about fourteen and had been hunting with these men since I could walk well enough to follow them.

By now all the dogs except one were nearly under our feet, making it difficult to walk. We were hunting with four mature plot hounds, weighing about seventy or eighty pounds each. Also along was a half grown pup, having fun and learning his trade. He was also the one that showed no fear, and took off in the direction of the scream. A plot hound is a large breed used in our area mostly for coon and groundhog hunting, but is also used for bear, boar, and mountain lion as well. Plots are usually known as a bold and totally fearless breed, but not this night. The dogs were a sorry sight, cowering beside us with their tails now tucked, except for the pup, who was now going full bore to investigate the scream.

We stood there and just listened for quite a while. There was only silence, except for the pup trotting up the hill. The leaves were very dry, and we would have heard anything move, as we could now hear the pup moving towards the source of the sound. Grandpa and Bill now started talking about what to do next. Just seeing these big dogs this scared made me want to go back the way we came, but the men I was with were not used to backing up, and this time would be no exception. The sound had come from directly in our path, and after ten minutes or so we started on up the hollow, my vote hadn't counted.

Grandpa had now adjusted our course a few degrees to the left, which would take us to the top of the ridge, but on the other side of the gully. This would be a steeper climb but would allow us to pass while staying several yards away from this animal. I always thought Grandpa led us on up the hollow so he wouldn't look scared, but adjusted course a bit, because he wasn't stupid, and had no desire to have a face to face encounter with whatever this thing was with a single shot 22 rifle and a pack of scared dogs as our only defense. I still had a lot of boy in me and could be as scared as I damned well pleased, and I wanted out of there real bad.

As we climbed the hill, we would stop occasionally and listen and could plainly hear the pup in the dry leaves and knew he was getting near the source of the sound. When we were nearly at the same level on the hill as this animal and maybe fifty yards away, we heard a deep-throated growl that lasted about five seconds. Shortly afterwards the pup returned, wagging tail as if he had had a great time. This growl was so low in frequency that it might better be described as a rumble and was very similar to the low frequency sounds elephants use to communicate.

I have since wondered if Bigfoot families could use this form of long distance communications. If they did, we probably wouldn't be able to hear them very far. Had this growl been any lower in frequency, I don't think a human could have heard it at all.

When we got to the top of the ridge and therefore out of the hollow, there was another scream that lasted about four seconds. This one was high-pitched and not as loud as the first. We were still within one hundred yards or so of this creature. The dogs now became much more relaxed, except for the pup, who thought the whole night had been great. We then went home without further incident.

I'll never know what this animal was thinking when he bellowed and growled, but it could have been, "I'M here. YOU need to be somewhere else," because they seemed like warnings to me. I am now about the age my grandpa was at that time and have spent thousands of hours in the woods. I have never heard another sound like that. I am sure I will never hear an animal sound that loud again unless I once again run onto the "BIG GUY."

In my lifetime I have thought I was in danger several times, knew I was a few times, but have never been that scared again, but what the hell, I was still a boy!

Encounter While Fishing

Eyewitness Account:

My name is Dwayne. I am 31, married, father of two and probably the most skeptical person around. I can usually find some reasonable explanation for ghosts, UFO's, etc., but I heard something when I was thirteen that scared me more than anything ever had before or since. I am an avid hunter and growing up in rural West Virginia have spent the majority of my time in and around the woods. Basically, I am no stranger to animal sounds.

Anyway, one night me and a friend went to an area lake at night to fish. We did this quite often in the summertime. We had been there for about 30 minutes when up behind us in the woods we started hearing what sounded like voices about 40 yards up. The first thought was, there's some guys in the woods talking loudly and kinda whooping it up, which would have been unusual in the first place. I kept trying to make out what they were saying, but could not. I could never explain this to anyone until I read a submission I had stumbled across while surfing. The person had written he had heard what sounded like people talking backwards. It hit me then that was EXACTLY what it sounded like.

As I was listening, I assumed that it must be people in the woods, but they must be further away than I thought since I can't make out what they are saying. It sounded like people talking loudly only I could not make out words. While listening to this, all of the sudden there was a hair raising, bloodcurdling SCREAM from just up the hill behind us. I cannot possibly explain how frightening this sound was other than to say my body went limp with fear. It felt like my legs were jelly. I looked at my buddy who looked as scared as I felt and asked him, "WHAT THE HELL WAS THAT?" He said, "I don't know, let's go." We left in an extreme hurry to say the least.

I have told this story to many people over the years and have always said that it must have been a screech owl, panther, etc., although I have never believed it to be any of these. I had never considered the possibility of a Bigfoot until reading other people's stories about hearing that scream and how terrified they were by it, did I think that could have been. I had always thought my story was just not that "exciting," until I read other stories where people had not seen anything, only heard that scream, did I think, okay maybe I'm not nuts. I have listened to the recordings that people have made and believe me, the scream that I heard was not that sound. It was intense! Just reading stories from other people 18 years later still gives me chills.

Sighting While Driving Near Franklin, 2016

Location: Route 33 near Franklin
Date: November 21, 2016

Eyewitness Description:
The creature was described as a large "object." The man told his wife that it was a bear when she asked him what was beside of the road, knowing that his wife didn't believe these creatures were real. His wife proclaimed that the creature was not a bear but a Bigfoot!

Before the couple could get a better look, it vanished into the dark forest. They were unable to photograph the creature and can only rely on the memory of their encounter. The couple stated that they are planning to investigate the sighting once they can obtain permission from the property owner.

The encounter with the Bigfoot took place around 10 p.m. and lasted only mere seconds. The couple described the Sasquatch as a black-haired, bipedal ape-looking animal that stood about 7 feet tall.

Sighting Near the Cheat River, 1951

Date: April 28, 1951
Nearest Water: Cheat River

West Virginia 1951 Sasquatch Report:
The witness was ten years of age and was walking on family property which straddled the Cheat River. On the other side of the river, a B&O Railroad line ran parallel to the river. Alongside the main railroad there was a "dinky" railroad and a storage building for railroad equipment and supplies.

The witness happened to look up at a large clearing on the side of the mountain behind the storage and saw a large hair-covered creature standing on two feet watching him. He was a few hundred yards from the animal, but he quickly determined it was too large to be a human, and not an animal known to him. He watched for several seconds as the creature stood staring at him, and then the boy wheeled and started home quickly.

After walking a few steps, the boy turned to look again at the spot and the animal was gone. He was immediately alarmed because he did not believe the animal could have traveled out of the large clearing and into the forested slopes above it in so short a period of time. He thought the animal may have been running toward him and using the storage building for cover as he did so. The boy then ran to his home and told family members about his encounter. When they went outside, they saw no sign of the animal.

Sighting in Berkeley County, 1970s

County: Berkeley
Location: Knipetown Road about seven miles down Route 11 North, approximately 7 miles north of Martinsburg and to the west of Route 11

Eyewitness Account:
It was back in the early 1970s, spring time, late at night around 2 a.m. I was out riding down this road that had a farm on one side and an apple orchard on the other. As I was driving there was some movement about two hundred yards in front of me going across the roadway from the farm to the orchard. When the animal looked in my direction the eyes had a glare from the headlights. At this time I got a real good look at it, about 8 to 9 feet tall, very heavy build, long lanky arms, long dark red hair, very long stride (about two and a half steps to cross road). If I was to guess his weight, it would have been around 4 to 5 hundred pounds. I was on a road with very little traffic (I was the only vehicle on the road at that time).

I got to admit, I was not a Bigfoot believer until that night. I didn't tell anyone about this because I knew they would not believe me. I was one of the chief officers in our local fire department at the time and I didn't want people to think I was nuts. Oh, by the way, I did get close enough to see what it was or wasn't. I know I was shaken up a bit and did not travel that road for a long time afterwards.

Encounter in Raleigh County, 2009

Date: May 2009
County: Raleigh
Location: near Shady Spring

Eyewitness Account:
My wife and I were riding an ATV about one mile from an abandoned strip mine. We came up over a small hill and approximately 25 to 30 yards in front of us and to the right of the trail stood a solid black creature, approximately 8 to 9 feet tall, standing behind a tree that was only about 8 to 10 inches wide.

I saw the creature first and my wife didn't notice it until I suddenly stopped the ATV and was trying to get it in reverse to turn around. She asked me what I was doing. I said, "look standing over there." When she saw the creature, she started screaming, "Oh my god, no, no, no, no."

I finally got the ATV turned around and left the area as fast as the ATV would run. My wife kept looking behind us to see if the creature was following us. Thank God it did not, but I still did not slow down until we were about two miles from the sighting area. I have totally lost interest in outdoor activities that I once loved due to this experience.

Sighting Near Cabwaylingo State Forest, 2004

Date: 2004

Eyewitness Account:
I live in a place that would not even be considered a dot on a map except for the fact that we have a State Forest there. Cabwaylingo, which stands for all the counties surrounding it, Cabell, Wayne, Lincoln, and Mingo, is a rather secluded park, full of wildlife.

I was bringing my daughter home from a dental appointment when we saw it. I was driving my mother's van, which sits kind of high off the ground, and had the headlights on since it was just a little past dusk. The first glimpse was of something walking, in a lumbering sort of fashion, on the side of the road next to the passenger's side of the van. It was a tan color and walked on two feet just like a human does. Its movements were slow and heavy, and it had to have stood a good 6 feet tall or more. I could see that it was covered with hair, but its body resembled a human being more than an animal.

My father seemed to think it was a bear walking on its hind feet. I can assure you, this was no bear! When the van got close to being beside the creature, it went over the edge of the bank off the road. I was somewhat amazed at what I saw, but it all happened so quickly that I wondered if perhaps I was seeing things. Apparently, my daughter, who by the way was sixteen at the time, must have been wondering the same thing, because at the exact same time we turned to each other and said, "Did you see that?"

After I knew that she had seen it too, I turned around in a wide spot off the road and went back to see if I could spot it with my headlights. Whatever it was, it was already gone. Where it went over the bank, it could have and most likely did go across a very small branch and into a hollow on the other side.

I am not sure what this was, all I know is that it was not human, yet it was not like any animal I have ever seen before! I never really believed in Bigfoot, and I am not very sure I do now. The one thing I absolutely do believe is that if you ever run into this thing, you will not soon forget it!

Sighting on I-64

Story Source: West Virginia Ghosts
County: Alleghany County, Virginia, 1 mile from the West Virginia line on I-64

Story:
A bi-pedal primate type creature that can only be described as, what some say a Bigfoot, was spotted in Alleghany County, Virginia, on I-64 about 1 mile from the West Virginia line near the Jerry's Run exit. Multiple motorists reported the large, hairy, ape-like creature in the ditch line. One motorist reported it was 7-8 feet tall and cleared the fence on the side of the road like it wasn't even there. The Virginia State Police, along with the Virginia State Game Warden, are investigating and says anyone encountering the creature is not to cause any harm or harass the creature in anyway and have placed it as a protected species.

Sighting in Lewis County, 1999

Story Source: West Virginia Ghosts
Date: 1999

Story:
The Black Thing in Lewis County.

This happened to me this past hunting season in the woods right close to my home. Keep in mind I have been hunting these woods for years. It was the first week and I didn't see any deer. I didn't even see a squirrel. The woods were strangely silent. I was very happy for this season for I got a new M-1 Carbine rifle and I wanted to kill a deer bad. But I had no luck.

It was day five of hunting season and I went out earlier than I usually do. As I was walking on the path, I seen something walking in the tree line. I slowly walked on ahead. But whatever it was it was gone, so I went on. I sat for hours and no deer showed up yet again. I stood up and I heard something coming out of the brush. I pick up my rifle and slowly backed up, thinking it was a deer. What came out was no deer. It had to be at least 6 or 7 feet tall with black fur and the eyes of this "Black Thing" still haunts my dreams even to this day. They were dark red.

Scared to death, I fired 4 rounds from my rifle right into the chest of this thing. It let out an unearthly scream and bolted back into the brush. Being a hunter, I could not stand to leave an animal wounded. I waited a good 30 minutes, then I went and looked for blood, but found none. I know I was scared, and I know the rifle is considered under powered but from that distance I could have not missed with four .30 caliber hollow pointed slugs to the chest. It would bring down anything or anybody for that matter. I don't know what I shot but looking stuff up on the net, it sounds like I encountered a Bigfoot or something close to it.

Now strange things have been going on around my home. My cows and other livestock are scared. My fences and gates are being torn down by something. If it is the same thing that I shot, you can bet the next time I see it I won't have the small rifle in my hands.

Sighting in Wood County, 2013

Here is an interesting Bigfoot sighting I found on thinkaboutitdoc.com. I have heard of this theory, but this is the first time I have heard an account like this from West Virginia.

Story Source: thinkaboutitdoc.com
Date: 2013
Think About It Sighting Report Date: July and October, 2013

Sighting Time: 1 p.m.
Day/Night: Day
Location: Wood County
Urban or Rural: Forest- Forests in the process of selective logging. Hardwood forest, hilly terrain. The area is semi-remote, adjacent to the Little Kanawha River Valley.
No. of Entity(s): 1
Entity Type: Bigfoot Creature
Entity Description: over 7 feet tall, long matted black hair/fur, bipedal, face which was similar to a gorilla.
Hynek Classification: CE-111 (Close Encounter 111) Close observation with animate beings associated with the object.
Duration: 4 minutes
No. of Object(s): 1
Height & Speed: -
Size of Object(s): 20-30 feet in diameter
Distance to Object(s): -
Shape of Object(s): sphere
Color of Object(s): white
Number of Witnesses: 2
Source: Email

Summary/Description:
My sighting was unusual as I had been asked by a friend to go with him to attempt to see a Bigfoot creature. The creature I witnessed was in fact the epitome of a Bigfoot, over 7 feet tall, long matted black hair/fur, bipedal, face which was similar to a gorilla.

Here is why I called my sighting unusual. The creature literally faded into invisibility as I watched it disappear. The creature faded in a manner which was exactly like the alien in the movie *Predator*. I suspected that this creature was interdimensional.

I live very near my sighting. Standing in my front yard, the treetops of the area where the creature was sighted are visible. Four months after seeing the Bigfoot, I was taking out the garbage after dinner in October. I saw a large white sphere rise slowly into the sky from the area of my creature sighting. It was silent and moving slowly enough that I had time to have my wife come out to watch the object continue to raise to an altitude of two to three thousand feet and move east. The object passed directly over us and began to increase speed. It then turned orange and became very, very bright, and then disappeared. It had become so bright before disappearing that it illuminated the surroundings as though it was afternoon in July. I am a trained military observer of aircraft. What I witnessed was not a conventional fixed wing or rotor aircraft. It appeared to be an orb approximately 20-30 feet in diameter. It made no noise during the sighting. However, we felt a pressure wave after the object disappeared.

Sighting in the Dolly Sods Wilderness, 2006

Location: Dolly Sods Wilderness
Date: August 2006

Eyewitness Account:
I had a strange incident in August 2006 that continues to bother me because I have no explanation for it. I was living in Elkins at the time with my wife's parents. I used to go into the Dolly Sods Wilderness area a lot to go hiking and to just spend some alone time. I had heard stories about the Dolly Sods and that Bigfoot was in there. I never paid much mind to the stories.

One late afternoon I was in the low part of the Dolly Sods at the Red Creek. The area is really beautiful but you can wander off the trail and easily get lost. It started to rain so I was heading back toward my truck. On my way I noticed something big move out of some thickets about 50 yards to my left. I stopped to get a better look with my binoculars. I waited until I saw more movement then aimed the binoculars in that direction. What I saw actually caused me to gasp.

I could see it very clearly. This monstrous creature stood at least 7 feet and had black hair all over. It was walking on two very strong legs that looked human. The body was like that of a racing dog. In other words, it had a very large chest and a small waist and hips. The arms and hands were huge and bigger than a powerful man. I couldn't see the fingers because it was carrying vegetation. The head was huge and covered in thick hair, but the face had an odd looking form. It was hard to make out since it was moving away from me, but the jawline did extend out from the rest of the face.

It continued to walk swiftly away from me but in the same direction where the truck was parked. I didn't know what to do and kind of stood frozen for several minutes. I started to quietly walk towards the truck when I heard something crashing through the thicket again. I stopped and knelt down, but I didn't see anything. Well, I had enough and wanted to get out of there. I started to run toward the truck and made it there in about 10 minutes. I quickly drove away and went straight home. I never went back to the Dolly Sods. I am very wary of the wilderness.

I contacted a couple of wildlife experts who probably thought I was crazy. I would have never believed it if I hadn't seen it. One of these guys did say that there had been a "wolfman" reported in the area back in the 1870s and that he had personally talked to a few people who claimed to have seen Bigfoot. This wasn't a Bigfoot in my mind.

Not long after that incident, we moved to Morgantown. I still enjoy hiking but I prefer to stay on the more pedestrian trails.

Sighting While Driving, 2011

An article supposedly from the *Tippecanoe Gazette* Newspaper in Ohio that Les O'Dell found on Cryptomundo.

Local Residents Spot Bigfoot In West Virginia

For decades its existence has been debated. Thorough searches have found no conclusive evidence. But a pair of Tipp City women reportedly have the definite answer as they claim to have seen Bigfoot. Terri Bessler and Crystal Krieger were driving through West Virginia when in the clear of day they spotted the behemoth mythical figure. It was walking up a truck ramp, off of the highway, up into the wooded mountains.

"It was huge, there is no way it was a person," said Bessler, owner of Midwest Memories. The figure was a solid shade of black and showed no definition of any clothing lines.

Krieger is in agreement that the ever-elusive Bigfoot was seen. "If it was a real person, it was the biggest person in the world. And where would they be going? There is nothing up there but woods," she said.

Unfortunately, Bessler could not tame her anxiety ridden hands enough to get a picture. By the time she maintained enough control of her phone to take one, they were around the curve and out of viewing distance.

The purpose of their excursion was to pick up Krieger's son Cody, a 2011 graduate of Tippecanoe High School, from North Carolina and bring him home for Thanksgiving. In the U.S. Marines, Cody is stationed at Camp Geiger for the School of Infantry. They were enjoying just a typical drive through the mountains of West Virginia, when Bigfoot was clearly spotted and could not be anything else. The women estimate they were less than half a mile away from the Sasquatch and its size was in no way proportionate to a human. Neither their vision nor judgment was impaired in any way. "We weren't sleep deprived or juiced up on caffeine," said Bessler.

They expect that not everyone will believe their story, but they are certain of what they saw and urge everyone to keep an eye out for Bigfoot next time they travel through West Virginia.

Sighting Near Seneca Rocks, 1998

Source: Tippecanoe Gazette
Written by: Mike Woody
Report was taken by the BFRO
Submitted by witness Scott Fadely on Monday, February 9, 1998.
Witness sees a large creature crossing the road

Year:1998
Season: Winter
Month: January
Date: Late January 1998
State: West Virginia
County: Pendleton
Location Details: The sighting occurred in Pendleton County, West Virginia, near Rt. 55 near Seneca resort area.

Observed:
I was traveling early one morning in January, in snowy conditions, when I spotted a large, upright, dark-colored creature just off Rt. 55. Very tall, fuzzy looking, with primate features, similar to an ape.

Also Noticed:
The creature stepped into the road, causing me to swerve to avoid colliding with the beast.

Other Witnesses:
I was driving

Environment:
Near Seneca Rocks, in the Seneca Valley; mountainous terrain; wooded; scarcely populated.

35th Star Publishing
Charleston, West Virginia
www.35thstar.com